CW01463901

• HALSGROVE DISCOVER SERIES ➤

HIDDEN RIVERSIDE NORWICH

HOW THE RIVER WENSUM SHAPED THE CITY AND ITS SUBURBS

STEVE SILK

HALSGROVE

First published in Great Britain in 2016

British Library Cataloguing-in-Publication Data
A CIP record for this title is available from the British Library

ISBN 978 0 85704 282 8

HALSGROVE
Halsgrove House,
Ryelands Industrial Estate,
Bagley Road, Wellington, Somerset TA21 9PZ
Tel: 01823 653777   Fax: 01823 216796
email: sales@halsgrove.com

Part of the Halsgrove group of companies
Information on all Halsgrove titles is available at: www.halsgrove.com

Printed and bound in China by Everbest Printing Investment Ltd

*This book is dedicated to Mum and Dad –
for all their encouragement over all these years.*

Contents

Ringland
River Wensum
Taverham
Drayton
River Wensum
Costessey
A47
River Yare
N
W
E
S

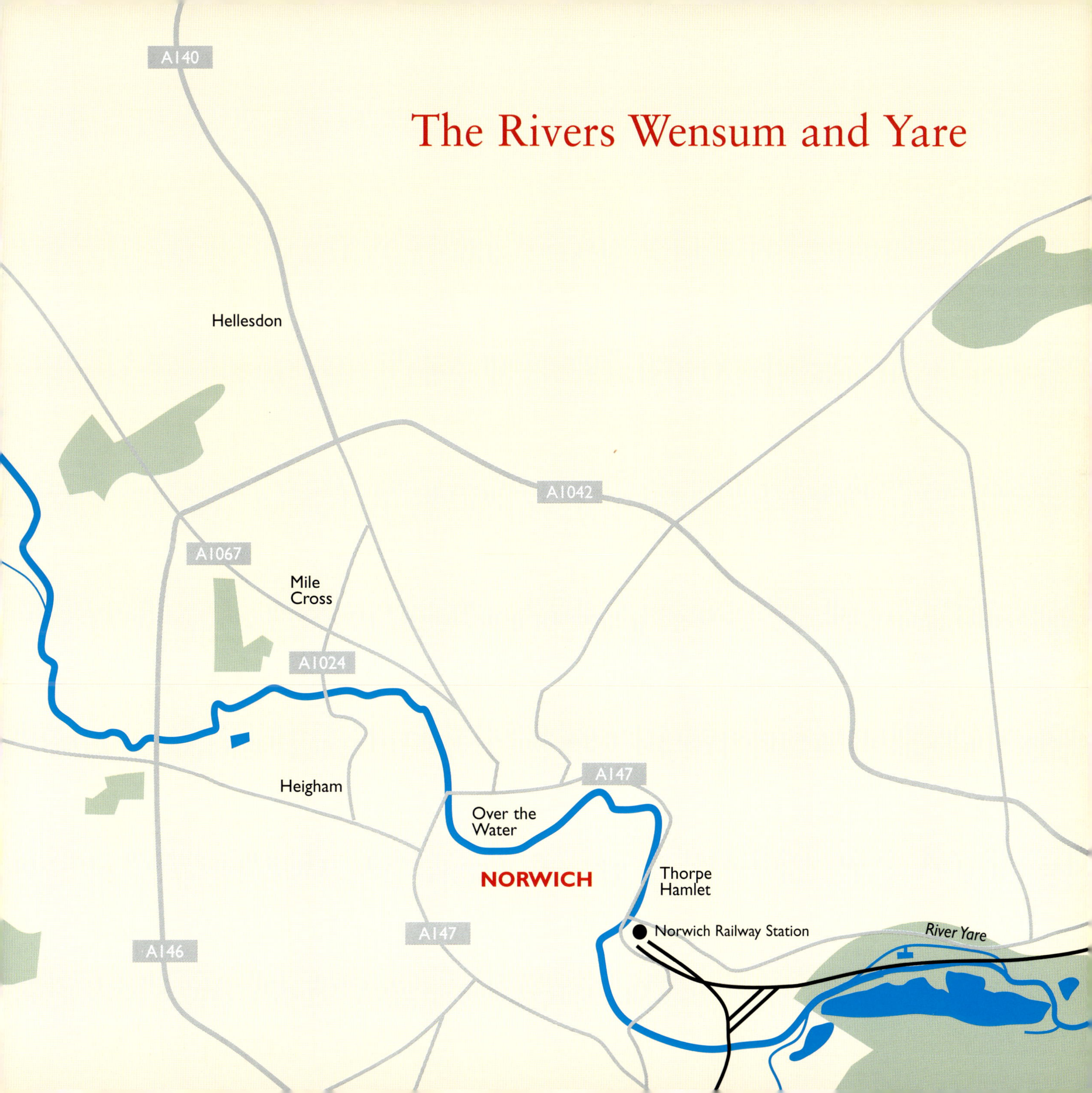
The Rivers Wensum and Yare
A140
Hellesdon
A1042
A1067
Mile Cross
A1024
Heigham
A147
Over the Water
NORWICH
Thorpe Hamlet
Norwich Railway Station
River Yare
A147
A146

Canoe view at Hellesdon

Introduction

NORWICH IS A wonderful city but for too long the river which has defined and defended it has been overlooked.

Given that the Wensum was once where the dirty coasters arrived and the dirty industries thrived, that is not entirely surprising. But those days have gone. The river is now cleaner and greener. And over the last 50 years wharves and staithes have been replaced by apartments and footpaths. Three pedestrian bridges have been built in little more than a decade.

Many of us have our favourite stretches. But even people who know Norwich well, can struggle to keep the Wensum's winding route in their heads. It pops up at Hellesdon bridge for example, but then disappears behind Heigham. It sidles furtively into the city centre near the Barn Road roundabout and doesn't really announce itself until at least Duke Street if not the top of Riverside Road. But all the while this beautiful, rare, chalk river is providing habitats for flora and fauna and valuable places of peace and quiet for the rest of us.

This book aims to put all the pieces of the jigsaw together – from rural Ringland, through the suburbs and into the historic city. By boot, bike or canoe, the Wensum is there to be discovered.

Steve Silk

From top:

The Wensum near Drayton

The river's newest bridge

Chapter 1 Ringland

Ringland's beguiling poplars

One spring day a little over a century ago an artist and his rag-tag retinue of assistants and horses made their way along Costessey Lane in the direction of Ringland. Spotting two attractive riverside meadows, their leader continued to the village to strike a deal with the landowner.

"After standing drinks at the Inn, I was quickly back with the key of the padlock which fastened the gate," he later wrote.

"The ponies were grazing and the van placed, whilst Bob put up his tent. Before I left them a wood fire was blazing and they were cooking steak with onions and potatoes bought on the road. Could this happen today? These two – Bob and Shrimp – lived like lords for weeks at very little expense; and nobody made such tea."

The author was Sir Alfred Munnings – one of 20th century Britain's most important artists. And the canvases he painted here of horses and ponies have given Ringland a sort of immortality.

Riverside Ringland

In paintings like "The Coming Storm" and "Shrimp Leading Ponies across the Ringland Hills", Munnings gorged on a visual feast of heath and meadow, gorse and gradient.

"In Norfolk I used to buy my various models about May and got the string of them together, take my man and gypsy boy and go with a caravan for the summer," he recalled.

He liked to paint outside – in the landscape he was capturing. Biographer Reginald Pound said "his Holland smock [would be] smeared with cadmium yellow expended in trying to capture the glory of the gorse".

You can see why he would have loved it here. Even today Ringland is as unspoilt a Norfolk village as you could hope to find. Norwich lies seven miles to the south east, but it might as well as be 77.

At its edges there are pockets of common land with timeless names like Hare Wash and Sheep Dip. At its centre there's The Street, a friendly, lazy thoroughfare with a magnificent church at one end and the river at the other.

The Wensum meanders in one direction from Attlebridge and then turns the other way to head towards Taverham. It's not terribly easy to walk along the river bank, but on a summer's day the village gathers and paddles at River Green, next to The Swan pub.

I love canoeing the stretch from Ringland to Taverham. The water is clear and the surrounding countryside stunning. It used to be free. But since 2012 the parish council has insisted that us outsiders buy a permit before we launch at River Green. It's only £5, but it's an unwelcome bit of modern bureaucracy in an otherwise timeless village. What would Munnings have made of it all?

From top:
St Peter's Church
A fine roof

St Peter's Church

Set on high ground looking down on the village, St Peter's is a mini masterpiece with its 13th century tower, fine clerestory windows and some spectacular stained glass.

And then there's the roof. The experts enthuse about the hammer beams enclosed with ribbed coving. Church expert Simon Knott calls it breathtaking.

"There are similar roofs at St Peter Mancroft in Norwich and Framlingham in Suffolk," he says. "Both much bigger churches, but neither of them has anything like the impact of the roof here."

The Mortlock & Roberts guidebook from the 1980s describes the church's exterior, before adding excitedly:

"The temptation now is to rush in and admire the roof with binoculars – and why not, for this is one of the most perfect small-scale roofs anywhere... Mancroft with its magnificence and daring commands our admiration, but Ringland roof – so small, so compact, is simply and inevitably beautiful".

But the final word goes to the church's own leaflet. St Peter's, it says, "exhibits the finest qualities of late-medieval grandeur on an intimate scale". Succinct and perfect.

Ringland Bridge

For decades – perhaps centuries - the residents of Ringland made do with a wooden footbridge across the Wensum. The records show that repairs to the bridge were paid for from the rent of a small meadow nearby.

The rise of the motor car meant something more solid was needed – although in the early 20th century vehicles could just about ford the Wensum. According to a display in St Peter's Church, drivers needed the help of a man called Elijah Abel who would tow vehicles across with a horse – for a fee of course.

Today's bridge was put in place in 1924 at a cost of £1,700. Certainly the last incarnation of the wooden bridge looks none too sturdy to modern eyes.

Ringland Bridge now…

… And then

PEOPLE – *Sir Alfred Munnings*

Sir Alfred Munnings (left) returning to old haunts on the Wensum at Costessey

Alfred Munnings was a whimsical, artistic genius who became famous between the wars for his paintings of horses. He was often eccentric and always the life and soul of the party. "If at the end of the evening he had insufficient money," said his biographer Jean Goodman, "he would present the landlord with a drawing offered with such confidence that it was invariably accepted as good currency".

His most high-profile years saw him capturing the colour and drama of the races at courses like Epsom and Sandown, where he was loved by everyone from the stable lads he joked with to the royalty who offered him commissions.

His links to Ringland go back to when this miller's son from Mendham in Suffolk was still finding his feet. His first job was very commercial; designing posters and adverts at a lithographer's in Norwich. It was while he was living in the city that he discovered The Falcon Inn at Costessey during a bicycle ride.

"Meeting a landlord who looked like one and just a ride [away] had opened up a new world with fresh ideas," he wrote in his autobiography. "My first short stay at The Falcon was only a feeler for my future painting on the Ringland Hills."

Those paintings came in the spring of 1910 when he left Norwich with a motley collection of caravans and carts, horses and ponies. Accompanying him was a man called Bob, who looked after the gear, and a teenager called Shrimp whom Munnings later described as an "utterably uneducated, wild ageless youth". These two, paid handsomely by Munnings, would set out each day to find a suitable spot for the outdoor paintings that Munnings craved.

Munnings described Ringland and Costessey as being "situated in one of the loveliest districts of all the pleasant country surrounding the old city." Of the Ringland Hills he wrote: "I developed a passion for the gorgeous blazing yellow of gorse in bloom."

Above: *The Union Jack – formerly The King of Prussia*

Right: *The Swan at Ringland*

Ringland's Pubs

Ringland used to have two pubs, one at each end of the village. Now only The Swan survives – no doubt its riverside location helps it continue to prosper.

Documents show The Swan was The Swan at least as long ago as 1836, but who knows how much longer some kind of tavern has existed on this site?

The second pub was at the other end of The Street and was originally called The King of Prussia – a harmless name for many decades. But then the First World War broke out. Soldiers ripped down the sign and the landlord decided that a name-change to the Union Jack might do wonders for trade. It remained a pub until the 1960s and is now a private house.

Finally there is one intriguing reference in the archives to a third pub. An 1827 document talks of a blacksmith's in Ringland "formerly a public or common ale house called The Wounded Heart". Now where on earth was that?

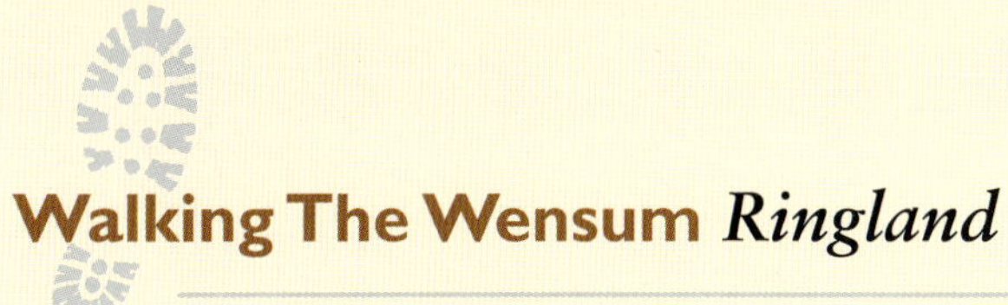

Walking The Wensum *Ringland*

Distance: 2 ½ miles

Unfold your Dereham & Aylsham OS Explorer map and take a close look at Ringland. Dotted green lines head out in every direction. This is a village that clearly believes in public footpaths.

Start at the church and head north-west along Ringland Lane passing the Reading Room on your left. This former Methodist Chapel was given to the village in 1964 by the Berney family. It has recently been refurbished with National Lottery money.

Take the first footpath on the right. The sandy track takes you up Royal Hill. From the brow look one way towards The Street in Ringland and the other towards the upper Wensum Valley and – higher up – the traffic snaking towards Norwich on the Fakenham road.

A right turn here will take you back towards the village centre, but press on as far as Low Farm on the edge of the Wensum's flood plain. From here river fans will want to make a five minute diversion to the Wensum itself. Head diagonally left from Low Farm crossing two tiny bridges. A more substantial bridge crosses the Wensum at a farm called Attlebridge Hall.

Now return to Low Farm and turn left at the gate. This path skirts the marsh dykes alongside Low Common. Watch out for geese, duck and snowy-white little egrets. As the path turns south, look across the river too. Our side is marshy meadows, the other bank shows the shiny greens and fairways of the Wensum Valley golf course.

The path then becomes Back Lane. Turn left along a footpath which emerges between houses on to The Street. Drinkers will want to turn left for beers at The Swan and perhaps a stroll down to the river again at Ringland Bridge.

Retrace your steps along The Street admiring Ringland's selection of houses ancient and modern. This road includes a dog-leg turn about half-way along its length. The house on the right hand side here was once the Union Jack pub.

Next look out for the flamboyant former school building, also on the right. This redbrick extravaganza dates back to 1873 and was built by the Berney family – historically the big landowners here. With its tall slender chimneys, the experts describe it as a "Tudor-Gothic hybrid". The school closed in the 1970s and has more recently been refurbished and extended. From here it's only a few hundred yards back to the church.

From top:
From Royal Hill
The bridge to Attlebridge
Ringland: footpaths in every direction

Chapter 2 Taverham

At first glance Taverham could be dismissed as a dormitory suburb full of people zipping Norwich-wards in a hurry. True, it has grown enormously in recent years and the overwhelming majority of the housing is not only post-war, but post-1960s.

But the old village didn't grow up around the Norwich to Fakenham road, it clustered around its ancient church, the nearby river and an important mill. Of course commuters pour down the A1067. But take a trip to the high ground and look the other way. The rolling acres of rural Norfolk seem much closer here than they do in Costessey or Hellesdon for example.

Certainly the village is steeped in history – so much so that it can claim its own saint. According to the legends, St Walstan tilled the soil close to the church and became the patron saint of agricultural workers in the process.

Close by, the Wensum executes a smooth anti-clockwise meander. Golfers at the Wensum Valley Golf Club look north and west to see a river heading in from the sticks. Visitors to the Taverham Mill nature reserve see a river already slightly tamer. It's only half a mile between the two points as the crow flies, but by canoe you would need to cover two and a half miles.

Opposite: *Canoe view near Taverham Mill*

Finally Taverham is hilly. From a high point 42 metres above sea level, the contours ebb and flow. The gradients will lessen and the river's meanders become less extravagant as we head towards Norwich. Yes, Taverham has a lot of cul-de-sacs and conservatories, but it likes to think it has a wild side too.

Winter at St Edmund's

St Edmund's Church

In 1862 a plan to restore the interior of St Edmund's church ran into trouble when plaster fell off a pillar. As the builders investigated, it transpired that the south wall was close to collapse and only one of the pillars was actually doing its job. Workmen had to be hurriedly diverted from another project to prevent 1,000 years of history from toppling down.

"The church was propped up while new foundations were dug," writes Judy Sims in her history of the church. "The pillars were rebuilt on their original bases according to archaeological evidence."

The work was paid for by Rev. John Nathaniel Micklethwait, who was the lord of the manor rather than the rector of the church. A rich man who owned most of the land in the village, he demolished and then completely rebuilt Taverham Hall at much the same time.

Today St Edmund's is a medieval church in a modern setting. Drive past the modern houses on Sandy Lane and it comes as quite a surprise. But of course this was the heart of the old village. Look closely and you'll see that today's four-way roundabout was once a six-way junction – the two extra roads heading to Taverham Mill and Taverham Hall.

St Edmund was killed by the Danes in 870AD, and experts agree that churches in his honour normally pre-date the Norman Conquest. The base of its round tower is probably from the 11th century while the octagonal top was added after a lightning strike in the 15th century.

Taverham Hall

Taverham Hall

Taverham Hall may be a preparatory school now, but it looks every inch the Victorian country house it was designed to be. Is it neo-Jacobean or neo-Tudor? The experts can't seem to decide. Let's agree that it's a distinctive slice of three-storey 19th century redbrick, bristling with gables, tall chimneys and a taller turret. The original plan by architect David Brandon included a much grander tower too. "Fortunately good sense prevailed and the tower was never built," says the school website demurely.

It was built in 1858–9 by the lord of the manor Rev. Micklethwait, replacing a substantial hall on roughly the same site. Was that earlier building the first Taverham Hall? We only know that an estate of 3000 acres certainly existed in 1623.

The wider estate has changed considerably over the years. According to landscape historian Tom Williamson, it developed into a landscaped park – rather than farmland – from 1783 onwards.

Taverham Hall became a prep school in 1921 when it was bought by the Rev Frank Glass for about £12 000. His school in Roydon near Diss had outgrown its premises. It appears to have flourished here ever since.

Its 100 acres provide an idyllic setting for around 270 pupils. The grounds run down to the Wensum – where children are encouraged to canoe in the summer months.

Amongst its old boys is the journalist-turned-politician Martin Bell.

"If the starting point is Taverham Hall, the finishing point can be anywhere you want," he enthuses in the school prospectus.

Marriotts Way

Marriotts Way

Commuters into Norwich from this side of the city have one major advantage – a car-free cycle path all the way. It's the route of an old railway and it's called Marriotts Way in honour of the Midland & Great Northern line's founding father William Marriott.

The route follows the trackbed of two of his branch lines. Starting at Aylsham, Marriotts Way heads west through Cawston and Reepham before an extravagant loop at Themelthorpe brings it into the Wensum valley at Lenwade. From here it picks up a separate branch line which once ran from Melton Constable to a long-defunct Norwich terminus called City Station. After Lenwade there were stations at Attlebridge, Drayton and Hellesdon, but not Taverham.

In all that's 26 miles of footpath and bridle way. And because the line hugged the river valley pretty closely, Marriotts Way is an excellent way to explore the first few chapters of this book.

As far as this chapter is concerned, the tree-lined path heads south-east from Attlebridge, cutting across Fir Covert Road and Breck Farm Lane before slicing through Thorpe Marriott and finally the main A1067 en route to the old Drayton station.

As well as commuters and pedestrians it's made for that first family bike ride. From stabilised toddlers to wobbly octogenarians, Marriotts Way welcomes them all.

The Midland & Great Northern Line

So why was there a line here in the first place? Good question, say the purists. Many railways started life as a means of linking a centre of population to London. Others connected major provincial cities. But the M&GN was part of a much wider patchwork spread across the vast acres of Norfolk and Lincolnshire without an obvious overall purpose.

If you were being harsh, you'd say that it specialised in providing villages with pretty little stations on pretty little branch lines which were neither strictly necessary nor economically viable.

To be kind, you'd say its east-west routes complemented the north-south network run (much more profitably) by the Great Eastern Railway. Farm produce headed west. Tourists headed east to stations with evocative names like Yarmouth Beach and Caister Camp Halt.

It took its name from the companies which jointly owned it – the Midland Railway and the Great Northern Railway. But famously it was better known as the Muddle and Go Nowhere line. Under the firm leadership of William Marriott it also had a reputation for being a model employer. Less well-known is the fact that we can't even blame Dr Richard Beeching – the 1960s railway rationaliser – for its downfall. The M&GN was so unprofitable that it was all but put out of its misery in 1959.

From top:

All quiet in Thorpe Marriott

The Otter

Thorpe Marriott

Until well into the 1980s, fields stretched as far as the eye could see between the Fakenham Road and the Reepham Road on the border between Taverham and Drayton.

But local planners had a vision, and a generation later an entire community has evolved, complete with pub, shops and a church. It has a village hall, even if some people don't regard it as a village. And now at least 8000 people live in the thoroughly modern Thorpe Marriott.

Like everything else about this charming mega-estate, its name was well-planned. The authorities held a competition. And from 36 submissions came the winning entry. Edwin Spalding of nearby Breck Farm Lane wanted to honour William Marriott, the founding father of the Midland & Great Northern Railway. The name works beautifully. Mr Spalding's prize? A bottle of champagne and £100.

Back in 1980 when the plans were still on the drawing board, this all seemed quite daunting. The 340-acre site was owned by 45 different people. Even once the land had been bought,

PEOPLE: *William Marriott*

The Midland & Great Northern Railway was in William Marriott's blood for more than 40 years. He arrived at what was known as the Yarmouth & North Norfolk Railway in 1881. Amalgamation followed takeover so that by the time the M&GN was born in 1893 he had held senior positions for a decade. He finally stepped down in 1924.

The 1880s was a time when railways were being built across the country, almost month by month. In Norfolk that meant a spidery spread of cuttings and embankments, much of the work directly overseen by Marriott himself.

"I loved the work of opening new ground and especially being in charge of the gangs of men," he recalled in 1921.

"Our railway was a boon to the agricultural labourer, who was then only getting about 12 shillings per week, whereas we usually paid about 18 shillings."

This new network created an unlikely junction in the previously tiny hamlet of Melton Constable. Marriott made Melton a railway town from scratch. It was hard to get people to move there, but he led by example and chivvied local builders into the construction of terraced houses. Difficult as it is to imagine now, Melton Constable was a hectic hub of locomotive workshops and goods sidings. It was, they said, the "Crewe of the East".

A stern, patrician sort of boss, Marriott prided himself on providing education for his staff. Every apprentice took classes in the company's time and then had to pass simple tests in reading, writing and arithmetic.

"Although the boys do not like being made to learn, yet in after years, grateful letters are received from them," he said.

Today he is remembered at the William Marriott Museum at the Holt terminus of the North Norfolk Railway. The NNR runs steam trains along a five mile stretch of another old M&GN line between Holt and Sheringham.

Museum curator Dave King points to Marriott's strong religious beliefs. "Temperance and religion were at the heart of everything he did," he told me.

"Apparently when apprentices passed out, he gave them each a Bible. Both Mr and Mrs Marriott believed they were trying to guide the men, to create a more rounded workforce."

Finally, Marriott ran a safe railway, in the era before Health and Safety won their capital letters.

"It has been for 41 years my constant prayer that God would during the time of my responsibility keep us from accident," he wrote to his staff when he retired in 1924.

"You all know that though scores of millions of train miles have been run, yet we have never had a serious accident to a passenger train or killed a passenger and many who read this will, with me, thank God for His mercy..."

He died in 1943.

work had to be shared among three building companies – and no-one thought they would work together.

But by December 1986 houses were up for sale – a four-bedroom Bovis home went for £82,500. By 1990 the development was confident enough to begin work on a village hall. Seven years later came The Otter pub. Because Thorpe Marriott was planned, the shops, the pub, the church and the village hall share a central square. A narrow green belt – complete with pond – exists too, alongside the old railway line.

Taverham Mill

A peaceful spot now, this section of the river once hummed with the non-stop industry of a paper mill. In fact the paper made at Taverham was amongst the finest in the country. It was used by *The Times* for its newspapers, the Bank of England for its bank notes and Oxford University for its dictionaries. According to the Taverham historian T B Norgate, the mill occupied more than four acres: at its height there were three water wheels helped by 11 steam engines.

"Towards the end of the last century," he wrote, "the output was 5½ reels of 72 inch wide dazzling white paper a day, without a blemish. Even the eyesight of some of the workers was said to be impaired by the glare from gazing at so much whiteness day after day."

There has been a mill on this site since Domesday, but there's little evidence of it being used to manufacture paper until 1700. Two centuries of success came to an end in 1899 when the last owner J H Walter announced he couldn't make it pay. He'd been defeated by distance from his markets, distance from the coalfields and rapid changes in technology.

Today little remains. To see the mill pond and weir you need to head to the Taverham Mill nature reserve.

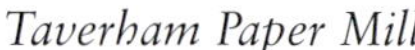

Taverham Paper Mill

Taverham Mill Today

If you're not a member of the local golf club or a pupil at the prep school, it's quite difficult to get close to the Wensum at Taverham. The best bet comes thanks to Anglian Water, on the site of the old mill, opposite the church.

From here you get access to ¾ mile of the Wensum as well as grazing marshes patrolled by particularly shaggy Highland cattle. Before 2014 the site was aimed squarely at anglers who try their luck in the lake and the pits to the south. The nature reserve only opened in 2014. And it does cost – £3 per adult at the time of going to press. The big draw for the fishermen remains the 22-acre lake known as The Mills, complete with otter-proof fencing.

The stone close to the visitors' centre is in memory of eight American aircrew who died when their B24 Liberator crashed into one of the lakes on April 21st 1944. The pilot and co-pilot were thrown from the plane. They were the only ones to survive.

The Silver Fox

The Silver Fox

This pub started life as two luxury caravans pulled up side by side. But given that Taverham's only previous inn had closed in the late 19th century, the locals weren't inclined to be fussy.

Today's building has a classic 1960s feel to it – local author T B Norgate dates it to 1968. It was named in honour of a silver fox farm just up the road at Walsingham Plantation. Within the woods, next to the present day Taverham Nursery and Country Shopping Centre, Major Anthony Carr set up his farm soon after the First World War.

"The basis of the industry, wrote Norgate, "was the production of pelts in the raw state to become furs ready to wear as stoles and capes.

"His pedigree stock, together with sound management, soon produced some outstanding animals which won several major awards."

Fur farming has long since been made illegal. But between the wars it was a niche industry. A 1930s leaflet produced by another fur farm in Sheringham talked of foxes kept in pens and being fed on raw meat – liver, tripe and rabbit. The animals were "ready for pelting" at 7 or 8 months old.

"Furriers state that the silver fox is above ordinary changes of fashion and that there is no possibility whatever of there being a glut of good quality skins," wrote its owner.

Top: *Honoured by two villages*

Above: *St Walstan with his scythe*

In that respect he proved wildly optimistic. After the war fashions changed fast. The last reference I can find to Major Carr's farm is in 1950. But thanks to Taverham's only pub, its memory lives on.

St Walstan – Taverham's Saint

Taverham has its own saint – a tenth century farmer known as St Walstan. The *Oxford Dictionary of Saints* is wonderfully dismissive of him, calling him a local saint "not known in any liturgical document". But whatever your views on medieval hagiography or modern history, you have to admire the legend's sheer durability.

The story begins in approximately 972 when St Walstan was 12. He walked the seven miles to Taverham from his home in Bawburgh, giving away all his possessions in the process. He took work as a farm labourer and, as the church guide, says "lived a life remarkable for its poverty, humility and charity".

After 33 years, he realised his time had come and received Holy Communion from a priest in the field where he worked. The spot became the first of three places where a spring miraculously appeared.

After his death, his body was borne by oxen which moved south towards Costessey Woods. Where they rested, a second spring appeared. St Walstan's latest biographer Carol Twinch pinpoints this well to just north of the A47 between Easton and Costessey Park. The oxen crossed the Wensum in the Costessey area, leaving wheel tracks, says the legend, which could be seen for years afterwards. The cart continued south to Bawburgh, resting in meadows close to the church. The third miraculous spring sprang up here. The curative powers of the water from this well were still being claimed as recently as 1927.

Carol Twinch does a super job exploring the twists and the turns this saintly legend has taken. Bawburgh church grew rich as a place of pilgrimage in the Middle Ages before the shrine chapel was destroyed during the Reformation. Without the shrine, the centre of gravity started to shift, as Twinch explains:

"After those walls had gone, a new outward sign was needed if the cult of St Walstan was to be seen to exist. Conveniently, Taverham, Costessey and Bawburgh all lay close to river beds and the legend of St Walstan was steeped in a tradition of springs. Had it not been the miraculous water of St Walstan's Well which pilgrims had sought in times of sickness; and had it not been to the well that local farmers had brought their animals? In the absence of the saint's mortal remains and without the machinery of organised religion, the well became the replacement focus for the legend of St Walstan in post-Reformation Bawburgh."

Today he survives as the patron saint of farm workers. And even the *Oxford Dictionary* acknowledges that the cult was "interesting as an example of veneration by humble folk of one who shared the same round of agricultural pursuits as themselves and had attained sanctity in doing so".

Certainly what the legend lacks in historical exactitude it makes up for in solid Norfolk geography. A thousand years on, most of the landmarks are still there to be discovered and explored.

EYE WITNESS: *St Walstan's Day 2014*

Can the medieval legend of St Walstan work for modern churchgoers? Every year parishes in Bawburgh and Costessey give it a good go. On June 1st 2014 Catholic churchgoers walked in pilgrimage from Our Lady and St Walstan at Costessey to the centre of Bawburgh. Joining their Anglican neighbours at the bridge, they walked to the village church of St Mary and St Walstan for a prayer service and a short ceremony at St Walstan's Well. The weather was perfect, the minister cheerful, the mood informal. After almost 1000 years of practice, Bawburgh clearly knows this ritual well.

Perhaps the secret lies in acknowledging that St Walstan's life story is mostly folklore and legend, but arguing that his example of quiet humility is pretty universal. The 60+ congregation heard readings and sang hymns, including one titled "Come Journey in St Walstan's Way". There were prayers for agricultural workers, the health of the environment and "our beloved county of Norfolk". At the well itself, the choir acknowledged its Yare-side setting with a "Down by the Riverside" spiritual.

Certainly the priest in charge is right behind her parish's most famous son: "St Walstan is a very significant figure in the life of the people of Bawburgh and further afield," the Rev Darleen Plattin told me.

"We are looking forward to commemorating the 1000 year anniversary of his death and the appearance of the well in 2016."

And us in the congregation? We trooped off to the neighbouring Church Farm for tea and cake – but only after the visiting preacher had judged the results of the bake-off. St Walstan's Day in Bawburgh continues to evolve, but as a tradition, it seems to be in rude health.

Above: *St Walstan's Well*

Left: *St Walstan's Day service*

Canoeing The Wensum *Ringland to Taverham Mill*

Distance: 6 miles round trip

On a summer's day River Green at Ringland quickly fills up with picnickers and paddlers. But within a hundred yards the canoeist leaves civilisation behind. The river winds left and a long row of elegant poplars demand to have their pictures taken, their trunks reflecting in the crystal clear water.

Then the Wensum begins a long lazy meander. Cattle graze the meadows to the left while horses are stabled on the right bank. In summer, if you're lucky, you'll hear cuckoos and see an occasional kingfisher. Banded demoiselle damselflies flit from leaf to leaf by the dozen.

Nature has provided a new bridge on this stretch. A poplar has fallen clean across the river, creating a dam to be by-passed. Further downstream the river gets more claustrophobic. Dodge and weave around low-lying branches of alder and white willow.

Costessey Lane gets closer in time to catch a view of the white-washed Beehive Lodge, originally a lodge for the long-demolished Costessey Hall. Then road and river diverge, leaving longer and longer gardens for the selection of static caravans and houses which lie undetected by all but us river-users.

Later the country becomes more open again. To the left, the grounds of Taverham Hall prep school, to the right, the Taverham Mill nature reserve. After three miles on the river, the sluices here mean our journey's at an end. Turn around in the slower water dominated by yellow water-lilies and head for home.

Opposite: *Canoe view: Beehive Lodge*

Right: *Taverham Mill sluice: time to head home*

Chapter 3 Drayton

Behind Wensum Valley Close

Clustered around a crossroads, Drayton always feels busy. In fact four other roads converge on the Drayton High Road as it heads towards Fakenham from Norwich. Dodge the traffic and you'll find that most of your needs can be met here. A bakery, a bank, two pubs, a garage, a small industrial estate and the mighty building firm R G Carter. Until 1959 the village had its own railway station too.

The church lies just to the north of the crossroads. "Steadfast and serene, watching over all" is how Madeline Checkland described it in her 1970 village booklet.

Check your OS Map and you'll see "Bloods Dale" marked between the High Road and the Low Road. It is said to mark the site of an old battle between the Saxons and Danes. Nearby the ruins in the grounds of Drayton Old Lodge also have a story to tell. Neighbouring noblemen clashed here in medieval times – and the building has the scars to prove it.

Canoe view: The Wensum near Low Road

The Wensum stays out of trouble to the south. Many a Drayton resident will barely set eyes on it. But head down to the Low Road where cul-de-sacs with names like Wensum Valley Close, Riverside Close and The Waterside rather give the game away. I particularly envy the residents of Wensum Valley Close. Behind their houses lie spacious playing fields running down to the river. Alder trees dip their roots at the water's edge and damselflies flourish in the heat of summer.

Finally a mention for an old psychiatric hospital, long since demolished. A distinguished Australian poet was among the many patients to receive treatment at the David Rice Admissions Hospital. The poems of Francis Webb are sometimes difficult to interpret. But I find it poignant and not a little haunting that some of the best writing inspired by the Wensum valley should have come from a brilliant yet fragile mind, thousands of miles from home.

St Margaret's Church

St Margaret's is one of the most spotless churches we'll meet on our long journey down the Wensum.

But it hasn't always looked this good. It was unloved for much of the first half of the 19th century – so much so that the church tower fell down in December 1850. With Victorian gusto, a renovation project was launched during which the nave and the chancel were also completely rebuilt. As a result, say the experts, this nominally 13th century church has a totally Victorian appearance.

St Margaret's: "steadfast and serene"

St Margaret's lies very close to Drayton's busy crossroads, but despite the traffic it still manages to feel secluded, helped by a substantial graveyard on one side and a well-tended playground on the other. This park was once the site of a large pond. Today nearby Pond Lane provides the only reminder.

Drayton Old Lodge: built 1914

Drayton Old Lodge

The Drayton Old Lodge estate may go back centuries, but the building we see today is dated very firmly to 1914. This stylish "Tudorbethan" mansion has seen a few different incarnations over its 100 years; private house, nursing home, health authority HQ and now a business centre and wedding venue.

For much of the 19th century the Old Lodge estate was owned by the Magnay family – well-known for running the nearby paper mill in Taverham. By 1912 they had sold it on to a Norfolk barrister returning to England after a successful career in Bombay. For £6000 Ernest Barkley Raikes bought the house, a farmhouse, five cottages and land which stretched beyond Low Road to the river. In the delightfully arcane old measurements it came to 83 acres, 3 roods and 24 perches.

By 1913 Raikes had drawn up plans to knock down the existing house. In its place came the much grander building we see today. Some wonderful architect's drawings survive in the Norfolk Record Office. Clearly no expense was spared; Portland stone in the hall, a massive billiard room to the right of a grand entrance, a drawing room to the left.

It all fits with what we know of Raikes – surely a man with a zest for life. He was born at Carleton Forehoe in Norfolk and attended the Haileybury public school before going to Oxford. He was called to the bar in London in 1898, married in 1899 and spent at least a decade at the Indian Bar in Bombay where he played first class cricket for a team called The Europeans. (In sport he was eclipsed by his remarkable brother. George Barkley Raikes played cricket for Hampshire and football for Corinthians and England. Oh, and he was a vicar too. Quite a combination.)

Ernest Barkley Raikes

But back to Drayton Old Lodge. Look up above the entrance and you can see a crest: EBR for Ernest Barkley Raikes and HR for his wife Hilda. Look at the date though. The house was built in 1914, on the eve of the First World War. Raikes wasn't to know, but the world of sculleries and servants' quarters wouldn't feel quite so natural by 1918. Drayton Old Lodge survived of course, but many grand houses really struggled in the more austere post-war climate.

And so to an afterlife. Dates are hard to come by, but I've seen photos showing it was the Drayton Nurses Home by 1938. By 1975 it had become the HQ for the Norwich Health Authority. And since the 1990s it has begun a slow metamorphosis into a business centre and wedding venue.

The Ruins

Built in a brick that's almost Disney-pink in colour, and set in the grounds of a wedding venue, you could almost believe that "The Ruins" were a modern folly.

"The Ruins"

In fact everything is old, genuine and fascinating. It looks like a mini-castle and it certainly used to have a tower in each corner, but the technical term is a "fortified house".

It was built in 1437 by Sir John Falstof – the man Shakespeare might just have modelled his "Falstaff" on. On his death it passed to the Paston family and became the centre of a vicious tug of war between the Pastons and the Duke of Suffolk. So while it's hard to imagine now, the Wensum was once the front line in a battle between the Duke across the river at Costessey and the Pastons in both Hellesdon and Drayton. Today, within the grounds of Drayton Old Lodge, it's a great backdrop for all those wedding photos.

Drayton's Pubs

While Taverham's single pub goes back to the 1960s, Drayton can boast two with a much longer lineage. The Red Lion and The Cock Inn have been in existence for at least 200 years. They overlook each other in the centre of Drayton, thriving in the 21st century as they did in the 19th and 20th.

Despite the pub sign, The Cock probably doesn't refer to a cockerel. The geography of Drayton means it's much more likely to refer to a type of horse – a cock horse. Norfolk blogger Joe Mason explains all on his "joemasonpage" website.

Below left: *The Cock Inn – until the 1950s*

Below right: *The Cock Inn today*

Bottom left: *The Red Lion during the First World War*

Bottom right: *The Red Lion today*

"These were horses used to aid heavy carts up hills, and Drayton Hill starts at The Cock and an equally steep hill going the other way towards Fakenham. Nowadays we have forgotten all about cock horses except in the old nursery rhyme "Ride a cock horse to Banbury Cross" – and we probably think this is just a bit of nonsense."

The present pub was built in the 1950s by the builder R G Carter who we'll meet later in this chapter. His grandfather had been the landlord. The building replaced a smaller, more traditional, inn on a neighbouring site.

The Red Lion dates back to the 17th century and is Grade II listed. The early photo here comes courtesy of Joe Mason and shows soldiers being called to order during the First World War. Head inside for a pint and enjoy the excellent selection of old photos of Drayton.

Drayton Cross

Drayton Cross

Restored in the 19th century, the medieval Drayton Cross now looks a little forlorn on a small green in the middle of a complicated crossroads.

"You who pray for the souls of William Beaumont and Joanna his wife, saying a Paternoster and an Ave Maria will earn a number of days pardon" was the message inscribed in French on the stone. The words have long been too faint to be legible, but today a translation lies on a plaque at the base.

But while the inscription tells us a lot about the complicated prayers-for-salvation mindset of medieval Christians, we know remarkably little about William and Joanna. The Drayton High Road was once part of an important pilgrimage route from Norwich to Walsingham. Presumably the cross was placed here in the hope of a high "footfall" amongst the pious heading north west.

Drayton Station

Opened in 1882, this was the second stop out of Norwich for the steam engines which once plied the Midland & Great Northern line between Norwich and Fakenham. It was also the biggest station and one of the busiest.

Full steam ahead at Drayton Station

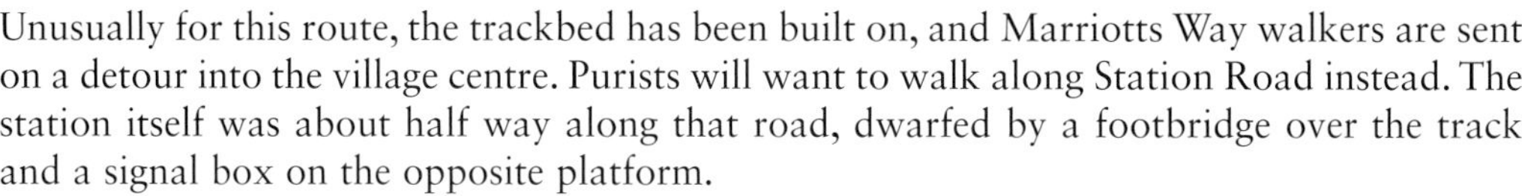

Unusually for this route, the trackbed has been built on, and Marriotts Way walkers are sent on a detour into the village centre. Purists will want to walk along Station Road instead. The station itself was about half way along that road, dwarfed by a footbridge over the track and a signal box on the opposite platform.

But the railway as a whole occupied many more acres. Today's industrial estate occupies the same footprint – a triangle of land on the corner of Station Road and Taverham Road. Old maps show this as a goods yard with at least six sidings and two goods sheds. The white railings we see to the left of this photo formed part of the cattle pens.

The station closed to passengers in 1959 and was closed down altogether in 1971. The buildings seem to have been demolished in about 1979. A modern industrial estate is of course a decent new use for a brownfield site. But it's a shame just one of those old buildings didn't survive to remind us of its past life.

R G Carter being raised by crane in his personalised lift to the top of the Norwich Union building in Surrey Street to inspect building progress in 1959.

RG Carter

It's no exaggeration to say that much of modern Norwich was built by R G Carter. The Drayton company has had a hand in everything from the Mile Cross housing estate to all four stands at Norwich City FC.

It's a remarkable legacy for a family firm which traces its roots back to one Robert George

Carter. He left school at the age of 14 to become a carpenter's apprentice with tools handed down to him by his grandfather. He served in the army during the First World War – winning the Military Cross and the *Croix de Guerre* for his bravery. After the war he set up his own business, building houses, schools and village halls. Many of the "homes fit for heroes" on the Mile Cross and Earlham estates were his work. Distinctive Norwich pubs like The Artichoke and The Gatehouse also bear his hallmark.

By the time R G Carter died in 1966, the company was comfortably the biggest of its kind in Norfolk. His son Bob Carter became chairman and by now the firm was involved in much grander projects. By 1971 it had a workforce of some 3000.

Bob Carter died at the age of 52 when his own son Robert was aged just 21. More than 40 years later Robert remains chairman, having seen his firm build everything from The Forum in Norwich to buildings on the Genome Campus in Cambridge. The firm has three main divisions; RG Carter Construction, Drayton Building Services and a property arm. A century after grandfather got going in Drayton, the R G Carter HQ remains in the village.

The David Rice Hospital Site

To the south of Drayton High Road, grassy fields fall away towards the Low Road and the river. One particular stretch is open to the public. Here, paths criss-cross the heath and dog walkers rule the roost. Only a clump or two of pampas grass look incongruous. Look closer and you might just notice the odd half-brick amid the sandy soil. This is the site of the old David Rice Psychiatric Hospital. It was built in the late thirties of the last century and demolished in the mid-noughties of this one. Who would have thought that ornamental plants would outlive the buildings they were designed to grace?

Once a hospital

David Rice had been a long-standing medical superintendent of the nearby Hellesdon Hospital. In an *Eastern Daily Press* obituary published in 1935, he was hailed as a pioneer who "will be gratefully remembered by many hundreds of patients who have benefited from his care". The hospital was built in his honour two years later. A 1938 plan shows it as rather spidery in shape – with wings heading off in all directions. Men were treated at one end, women at the other. It appears to have remained in operation until the early years of this century, before being demolished in around 2004/5.

Now owned by The Lind Trust, the 33 acre site was going to be home to a massive new church. Plans fell through after an acrimonious row with many local people. Trustee Graham Dacre now plans a small development of "less than 20 houses" on the wooded area close to Drayton High Road while the rest of the land would remain open for us walkers.

PEOPLE: *Francis Webb*

Francis Webb is one of Australia's most famous poets. But rather unusually some of his best poems are about a land far from home – the Wensum valley.

He's all but unheard of here. So those who know the landscape are unlikely to know his poems – and vice-versa. This "disconnect" is all the more poignant when you realise the reason for Webb's close association with places like Costessey and Hellesdon was a serious and chronic schizophrenia.

Webb was born in Adelaide in 1925. Plans to study at Sydney University were interrupted by the war and he served with the Royal Australian Air Force between 1943 and 1945. He published his first volume of poems in 1948 and visited England for the first time in 1949. Soon afterwards he was placed in an asylum after a suicide attempt, before returning to Australia the following year.

What interests us is his second visit to England – a seven-year spell between 1953 and 1960, the second half of which was spent in Norfolk. Not all of that time was happy, he was often a patient at the David Rice Hospital. But in that no-man's land between genius and breakdown, there's no doubt that he found inspiration from his immediate surroundings.

From the surviving belfry tower on Costessey Park Golf Course to "slithering yells of children on the sand-slopes" of Mousehold Heath, it's strange to see Norfolk through the eyes of an Aussie more than half a century ago.

Stranger still, because many of his poems aren't easy to fathom. His great champion in this country is Cameron Self of the Literary Norfolk website. Self describes his works as "complex, challenging pieces which blend location and intense poetic vision." Others, he admits to my relief, are "quite impenetrable".

Webb later returned to Australia and died in a psychiatric hospital in 1973. After many years of complete obscurity here, his star is now starting to shine a little brighter. A new edition of his poems was published in Australia in 2011, although it's still difficult to get hold of in this country.

A troubled soul writing often melancholic verse in a forgotten hospital, it's far from being a happy-ever-after story. But somehow what Self describes as Webb's "dense and muscular language", adds to the grandeur of Costessey and Drayton. A big literary name sought solace here and immortalised some of its nooks and crannies as he did so.

• *Collected Poems – Francis Webb edited and introduced by Toby Davidson, UWA Publishing*

Gale Force – Francis Webb

With rumbling brilliant barrow-loads devise
Temple and tower of cloud upon the sky,
Let the brave arch, the column fall and rise
With engrossed genius of your slavery.

My hill is strung with your vast breath and strain,
Coils of elation tumble down to earth,
Green fills the mullions of a phantom rain,
Eternal lightning heaves and travels forth.

The Wensum with a royal nonchalance
Shepherds his slender waters, yet the vision
Of vaster, upstairs doings takes his glance,
Patterns break out on humdrum ways to ocean.

You tell me all are as the leaping fish
And his silver devoted ripples, all are one.
Slave, power, your creative force and wish
Inform with praise the clouds, the earth, the sun.

The Wensum Valley at Drayton

Bloods Dale

The land climbs steadily from the Wensum between the Low Road and the High Road in Drayton. A footpath bisects the two roads and just to the north lies an idyllic spot at the centre of a grisly legend.

It's a long, irregular-shaped field with the unlikely name of Bloods Dale. And local tradition maintains that this was the site of an epic confrontation between the Danes and the Saxons. "In a plantation near the road are traces of an entrenchment; and at a short distance is Bloods Dale, said to be the scene of a battle in the Saxon era," wrote one Victorian chronicler. Everyone says "said to be". No one has the remotest bit of evidence, but tantalisingly 13 skeletons were dug up a short distance from here by navvies digging the Midland & Great Northern railway line in the 19th century.

All that we can be sure of is that the "Bloods Dale" name has a long lineage. A 15th century document talks of land called "Blodeshille" and "Blodisdale" owned by a Walter Nich of nearby Taverham. The first edition of the OS map from 1884 shows it as a large field running from Low Road to the brow of the hill, while a 1913 edition adds the wood we see today.

So if there was blood, could there still be treasure? According to the landowner John Ketteringham, the legend attracts modern day treasure-seekers - metal detectorists.* So far, sadly, they've yet to find more than the odd coin.

Finally look again at your OS Explorer map. Bloods Dale is picked out from the dozens of other field names the cartographers could have chosen. Well done Ordnance Survey for helping to keep this faint historical whisper alive down the centuries.

**Metal detectorists only allowed with permission of the landowner.*

Bloods Dale – a grisly legend

Canoeing The Wensum *Drayton to Hellesdon*

Distance: 2 miles

Best experienced as an evening paddle, the river between Drayton and Hellesdon is wonderfully tranquil. There's no obvious launch point, so I end up dragging the canoe down the wooden steps at Drayton Green Lanes. A vast willow tree has split asunder here. Its overhanging branches demand a bit of dodging and weaving, but then it's out into open country with the evening sunlight casting shadows from the west.

That Costessey bank gets steeper and you might make out Marriotts Way cyclists on the top of the ridge. Otherwise there's nothing in the way of human habitation to be seen. Meanwhile on the Drayton side we soon rub up against the houses off Low Road. Ever more expansive and expensive gardens follow, many with their own staithes and summer houses. I never see anyone, but it's the kind of spot which demands the drinking of G&Ts.

Costessey remains invisible to the right, but the tall white chimney of Briar Chemicals comes and goes on the Hellesdon bank. Houses tiptoe closer to the river. Beyond them you might make out the leaded spirelet of St Mary's church. Then, rather suddenly, you're at Hellesdon Mill. To continue towards Norwich do some quick portage on the west bank and drop into the River Tud which joins the Wensum here, just south of Tud Sluice. Otherwise, turn around and head for home.

Drayton Green Lanes

Chapter 4 Costessey

The suburban sprawl of Norwich has almost swallowed up Old Costessey. Almost. While New Costessey to the south is full of chalet bungalows and cul-de-sacs, its neighbour feels older and wiser. Dig deeper around the triangle of roads formed by The Street, Folgate Lane and Town House Road and you'll find two rivers, a Catholic tradition and the last remains of a "fairytale castle" called Costessey Hall.

Just about all of this historic manor house was demolished following the Great War. You need to be a golfer to see what's left – a ruined belfry block guarding the fairway on the 18th hole at Costessey Park Golf Club. Costessey Hall was built by the Jerningham family who were granted the manor during the reign of Queen Mary. They stuck to Catholicism through thick and thin, later providing a Catholic school and church in the middle of the village. To this day most old Costessey families are either Catholic or have Catholic roots.

And so to the rivers. Old Costessey lies between the valleys of the Wensum and its tributary the Tud. The Wensum's meanders provide the village's boundaries to the west, north and east while the Tud divides New and Old Costessey to the south. It's not obvious at first glance, but Costessey's development is still dictated by the waterways which all but surround it.

Finally for newcomers, it's pronounced "Cossey" not "Cost-essey".

Costessey Hall

Costessey's great tragedy is that its stately home was allowed to be demolished after the First World War. A building dating back to Tudor times went under the wreckers' ball in 1920. Ironically many of the walls proved so solid that they couldn't be knocked down: the remains were left to rot. One tower hung on for a further fifty winters before crumbling during a storm in 1971. Now only the Belfry Block remains, providing a dramatic vista at Costessey Park Golf Club.

But let's start at the beginning. In 1553 Sir Henry Jernegan was a Catholic knight under a Protestant king – Edward VI. But when the teenaged Edward died, Sir Henry was one of the first to back the cause of the Catholic Princess Mary. Indeed according to Costessey Hall's historian Ernest Gage, without the help of Sir Henry and other Catholic gentry "Mary's chances of being crowned queen in 1553 would have been seriously lessened". Two years later, the new queen rewarded Sir Henry with the manor of Costessey. And there, on the south bank of the River Tud, he built his new manor house.

But then the religious tide turned. Mary died in 1558 to be succeeded by the Protestant Elizabeth I. Thereafter to celebrate the Catholic mass was to commit a crime. So Sir Henry built a secret chapel in the attic of his new house. "This chapel was so cunningly contrived,"

Opposite: *Canoe view: heading down to Costessey*

Costessey Hall: demolished in 1920

wrote Gage, "that at very short notice, the altar, pulpit and pews could quickly be transformed to represent ordinary articles of bedroom furniture."

Later generations of the family became Jerninghams rather than Jernegans. And by the early 1800s Sir George William Jerningham and his wife Lady Frances were building "a prodigious hall with battlemented walls, towers and ornate pseudo-Tudor windows" to complement the older building.

Costessey Hall's demise was caused by the death of FitzOsbert Edward Jerningham in 1913. For inheritance reasons, the surviving member of the Jerningham family received the contents while the building itself passed to a different relative – a Lieutenant Colonel Fitzherbert in Staffordshire. Then the First World War intervened and the house was commandeered by the army.

Many stately homes suffered indignities during the war, but without a local lord to pay attention, Costessey Hall was particularly badly hit. Afterwards Fitzherbert put the entire estate up for sale and the surrounding farms were quickly sold to their tenants. But in an England exhausted by war, no one had the time or the money to invest a fortune on a badly bruised manor house. It was sold to a firm of demolishers. A stately home packed with history was knocked down for a knock-down price.

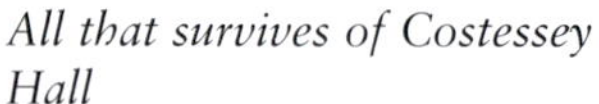

All that survives of Costessey Hall

PEOPLE: *Michael Fitt and Costessey Hall*

Photographs, paintings, even tapestries of Costessey Hall dominate the walls of Michael Fitt's living room. This former blacksmith grew up in Norwich Road, Costessey in the 1940s and has been fascinated by the Hall since the age of seven.

"I can remember seeing a couple of photos of it for the first time and thinking it must be a fairytale castle. Well, you would do at that age wouldn't you?"

The hall had been pulled down some 20 years before he was born, but that hasn't stopped him from following the building's afterlife with interest. He remembers being told that vandals were breaking into the family vault on the site in the 1950s and disturbing the bodies.

"In the end the police came down to protect them until they were moved. There were 32 bodies in all I think. And all us boys were sitting on the wall at the Catholic church when they dug a big hole to re-bury them."

A plaque in the churchyard records the precise date – November 18th, 1953.

When we imagine a grand building being demolished, we tend to assume it had long since fallen into disrepair. And true enough the soldiers who occupied Costessey Hall during the First World War did do some damage. But Mr Fitt's research has established that this was a building which was in its prime. Indeed it was still a work in progress. Ornamental wooden panelling lay completed but unfitted inside the building: bay windows were being added as late as 1910.

Perhaps that helps explain why so much of the fixtures and fittings were later re-used. A fireplace found a new home at Hethersett Hall, stained glass from the adjoining chapel travelled right across the country, and everything from balustrades to coal scuttles are being used in Costessey houses to this day. Just as the demolition men found it impossible to knock it all down, in many other ways Costessey Hall never quite disappeared. And Michael Fitt has done his bit to make sure those memories linger on.

Catholicism In Old Costessey

In a society which is becoming more secular, it's intriguing to discover that Catholic heartlands can survive in the most unlikely of places.

Historically, Norfolk is overwhelmingly Protestant. And yet there is a strong Catholic tradition in Costessey thanks to the whim of Queen Mary almost five hundred years ago. She rewarded Sir Henry Jernegan for his loyalty with the manor of Costessey and his descendants would exert their considerable influence here for more than 300 years. In the words of one academic writer in the 1960s "Old Costessey became an introspective Roman Catholic enclave in a Protestant region".

Costessey Hall chapel

It's difficult to say how many people stuck to the old faith here during the age of martyrs and priest holes. But once Catholic emancipation got underway in the 19th century, we see how quickly influential Catholic gentry could move. By 1809 a Catholic chapel had been built as part of Costessey Hall. (Incidentally stained glass for this chapel was collected from all over Europe for what appears to have been a sumptuous building.)

By 1821 a Catholic school had been built with land provided by the family. Enlarged and extended, it remains the only school in Old Costessey – a rare Norfolk example of where the village school is a Catholic school.

By 1834 the estate chapel wasn't big enough for a growing congregation from the village. Again the Jerninghams obliged, providing land for a church in the middle of the village. True, fund-raising for Our Lady and St Walstan's took time and the church was not completed until 1841. But almost 175 years later the building is still going strong and has recently been given Grade II listed status.

ARCHIVE: *A Royal Grant*

I like document JER244, 55X1 from the Norfolk Record Office. It might come in an anonymous pale blue folder, but inside the centuries fall away. Unfold the creased parchment, gently handle its saucer-sized seal and marvel at the 1500-plus words of closely hand-written Latin.

Its royal provenance is clear enough. It is in the name of "Phillipus et Maria" and there's a regal portrait of the pair written inside the giant first P of Philip. "Vivant Rex et Regina" runs the banner over their heads – long live the king and queen.

The document grants the manor of Costessey to Sir Henry, rewarding him for his early loyalty to the new queen. The Latin is beyond me, but apparently it comes complete with explicit recognition of his service "in the putting down of the rebellion of John, Duke of Northumberland, and other rebellions". Four hundred and fifty-odd years later, this legal document looks almost as good as new.

St Edmund's Church

Architecturally, the most interesting aspect of St Edmund's Church is its tower. What was clearly conceived as a traditional square of Norfolk stone ends abruptly after perhaps 50 feet. Then a totally incongruous red brick tower takes over. In the words of the online church expert Simon Knott the brick section "looks as if it might be on a visit from southern Europe". It's the wrong size, the wrong height and it's made of the wrong materials. A lead covered spirelet finally gives the building some dignity and some height.

But perhaps we're lucky that this church has survived at all. Because in the Elizabethan age it was deliberately abandoned as the nearby Jernegans exploited a legal loophole. Catholic estate workers had to attend their local Church of England place of worship *unless* that church wasn't fit for purpose. Neglect followed neglect to such an extent that the church nearly fell down. What we see now is largely the result of 19th century restoration.

Costessey Mill

There had been a mill at Costessey since Norman times. Goodness knows how many different wheels the Wensum has turned here over the centuries. In its last incarnation from 1858 it was a five-storeyed brick-built monster which must have dominated the surrounding countryside. It was powered by steam as well as water and the Norfolk Mills website describes it as one of the largest in the county. The building was reduced to a shell by a fire on July 7th 1924. Nothing remains of the mill itself, but the mill house, also built in 1858, survives on the Costessey side of the river. The existing weir dates back to the 1980s.

New Costessey's "Chinatown"

What happens when a large estate like Costessey Hall is sold off to a variety of bidders in a hurry? The answer in Costessey was a modern town planner's worst nightmare. The grounds and fields of the massive estate quickly became subdivided into dozens of small plots. People began building with whatever materials were available. Dirt tracks sprang up. They would later be dignified with proper names like Kabin Road and Hill Road. Converted railway carriages were a particular favourite for rudimentary houses and much of what would become "New Costessey", began life with nicknames like "Chinatown" and "The Back of Beyond".

From top:
St Edmund's Church
Costessey Mill: later gutted by fire
Early days in New Costessey

It all seems a world away from today's neat bungalows, but Gunton Lane resident Roy Howard remembers it well: "Costessey had a bad reputation in those early days. It was all wooden shacks. You could buy a bit of land for £50 and you put up what you could. The roads weren't made up and you got your water from a water pump."

The reason? Grinding poverty of course. Roy is remembering the 1940s, but the first people settled here not long after the First World War. While Norwich was one of the leaders in providing council houses, not everyone was provided for. Faced with the choice of a slum in the city or a new start in Costessey, many felt they had no alternative. It took a generation to shrug off a reputation for being poor and shabby, but slowly New Costessey smartened up its act. Over the decades the carriages were carted off and the roads were surfaced. Nowadays you have to be at least 65 to remember when it was any other way.

Old Costessey's Pubs

Where once there were six, there are now just two pubs in Old Costessey – The Harte and The Bush.

The Harte is perhaps the more obvious, occupying a prominent position on Costessey's major junction. There has probably been a pub on this site for 200 years, although the present mock-Tudor building dates to 1931. Until very recently it was known as the White Hart.

The Harte

The Bush

The Bush is tucked away down The Street. It backs on to River Wensum and provides an excellent launch point for canoes. A century ago it was known as "the infamous Bush Inn, frequented by prostitutes". I stress that was 100 years ago.

The most famous of the former pubs is The Falcon, some distance down West End. Now restored and whitewashed, it is known as Falcon House. The artist Sir Alfred Munnings stayed here for several weeks while he painted the nearby Ringland Hills. The Falcon was also the headquarters for the Cossey Gyle – a traditional village procession, or "country frolic" which survived until early into the last century.

According to Costessey's historian Ernest Gage, the other pubs were The Red Lion on West End and The Old Black Swan on The Street. The Roundwell, some distance from the village centre on the corner of Longwater Lane and Dereham Road, survived the longest. The building was demolished in 2010 to make way for a medical centre.

RIVER RESEARCH: *The Tud*

We can't leave Costessey without mentioning the village's second river. The Tud starts life to the south of Dereham and heads west through Mattishall, Honingham and Easton. It then goes on to divide New from Old Costessey before joining the Wensum at Hellesdon Mill.

The Yare heads in to Norwich from the west, while the Wensum winds down from the north west. And, in between, the 15-mile long Tud largely goes under the radar. Costessey people know it as the river which runs beneath Longwater Lane. It proved an irresistible spot for Sir Henry Jernegan when he built Costessey Hall alongside it in the 16th century. The present-day Costessey Park Golf Course looks all the better for its presence too.

Finding the source of the Tud is beyond the bounds of this book. But on a sunny September Saturday I couldn't resist giving it a go. The map shows the thin blue line running out at Spurn Farm on the southern fringes of Dereham. And the only way to find out more is to knock on the farmhouse door.

It's only recently that I've realised that this sort of thing scares the living daylights out of a lot of people. But I'm a newspaper journalist by trade and I love it. It reminds me of working on my first weekly paper in the Yorkshire Dales. Go in with a smile on your face and you'll always get a story, they told me. And they were pretty much right.

At Spurn Farm I was greeted by two black labradors and retired farmer Sue Haney who quickly assured me that yes, I was in the right place. She was kind enough to take me down to a modest channel of water, one end of which is known as "the little watering hole". It's not a spring, it's not pretty and Sue talks of other field drains coming in from other directions. But yes her family, who have farmed here for three generations, see it as a source of the River Tud. (She was quite insistent on "a" not "the".)

But "a source" is good enough for me. Another minor mystery is solved. Thanks Sue.

The River Tud at The Red Bridge

A Tud source

The Bike Ride *Costessey*

Distance: 4 miles

Start at the small car park off the wonderfully pot-holed Gunton Lane. Take Red Bridge Lane down to the River Tud and continue to Marriotts Way. Just before you reach the main path, turn left on to a sandy track. This bridle way heads uphill offering views to Hellesdon to the right.

Once you get to the top of the hill, Drayton replaces Hellesdon on the horizon. Keep right at the fork and you rejoin Costessey proper on St Edmunds Close. Turn right on to Folgate Lane and then right again on to The Street where St Edmund's church is almost immediately on the left.

The road now heads steadily downhill to where Costessey Mill once stood. Keep left to cross the Wensum and follow Costessey Lane which soon turns northwards towards Drayton. Take a right turn soon after the Brooklands Nursing Home to head up on to Marriotts Way.

You cross an old railway bridge here, offering a rare high view across the Wensum. We're now on the home leg and you can look right to see the outward bound route on the higher ground. Note the four mile (from Norwich) marker. Turn right at the three mile marker back on to Red Bridge Lane.

Chapter 5 Hellesdon

Historically, Hellesdon clustered around St Mary's church close to the River Wensum. A bridge has spanned the river here since at least the 16th century, while a mill had ground flour – on and off – for even longer.

But when the railway station opened in 1882, Hellesdon started its slow transformation into a commuter suburb. The Midland & Great Northern railway line offered an easy route into Norwich and encouraged people in the other direction too. A golf course on Rabbits Hill would soon blossom into the Royal Norwich Golf Club. (In the next few years the golf club will move even further out of Norwich, allowing Hellesdon to become yet more suburban, as new houses get built on old fairways.)

Until Victorian times the hamlet of Hellesdon had marked the limit of Norwich's borders. But from the beginning of the 20th century, new housing spread north and east. The old Hellesdon began to be called Lower Hellesdon while a new Upper Hellesdon flourished along the Drayton and Aylsham roads. Hellesdon Hospital began to provide employment. An outer ring road and new bus routes completed the transformation. But take a close look at modern-day maps and you will see that the boundary still exists. Lower Hellesdon pays its rates to Norwich City while Upper Hellesdon comes under Broadland District Council.

Largely avoiding the hustle and bustle, the Wensum forms Hellesdon's western boundary. The old M&GN line – now Marriotts Way – hugs that valley too. It allows cyclists and pedestrians to get into Norwich quickly and provides the perfect gateway for the rest of us to explore the many different faces of Hellesdon.

Hellesdon Bridge

It's an elegant bridge to canoe under, and a moderate pain in the neck for motorists to drive over. The cast-iron Hellesdon bridge was built in 1819, but it is only wide enough to take one car at a time. Even cyclists and pedestrians struggled, so in recent years they have been diverted on to a more functional footbridge alongside.

Hellesdon Bridge

Opposite: *Hellesdon's A-frame bridge*

From the footbridge, look out for the plaque marking the 1912 flood level. Considering the vast meadows upstream, the sign is amazingly high. If you can get down to the water's edge, look out for the signs directing river traffic too. "Keep this side going upstream" says one. It's witness to a time (just over a century ago) when this was a popular spot for rowing.

Bridges here have marked the boundary between "City" and "County" since at least the reign of Mary I. Norwich had won its independence from the county of Norfolk in 1404, but it was in 1556 that the city fathers finally spelt out the extent of their jurisdiction, including borders from Cringleford Bridge to:

"the outward bank of the river to Heilesden bridge and from thence to the water of Heilesden old watermill-damme and from that water by the highway leading directly through Heilesden town by the common lane, leading from the east part of an inclosure called Heylesdon-Wood..."

The bridge also played a cameo role in Kett's rebellion in 1549, during the reign of Mary's predecessor Edward VI. Refused entry to Norwich from the Cringleford direction, they headed north, crossing the Wensum at Hellesdon before swinging round to Mousehold Heath. Even then, we are told, Hellesdon bridge was so narrow that the rebels had to "supplement it with a rude causeway improvised with tree trunks and faggots"...

...which might or might not be a comfort to today's rush hour drivers sharing the same frustrations almost 500 years later.

St Mary's church: "tall for its size"

St Mary's Church

In 1970 the village of Hellesdon came together to celebrate the 600th anniversary of its medieval church. Less than 50 years later, parishioners are wondering whether they might soon celebrate the 1000th anniversary of a Saxon one instead.

It is the same church. It's just that the latest evidence suggests that the nave and the chancel are much older than previously thought.

"It is possible that they form the church which was in existence in the time of Edward the Confessor," writes Freda Wilkins-Jones in her history of the church.

The best guess, she adds, is that some sections were built between 1040 and 1120. So what was once considered 14th century, is actually more likely to date from either the late Saxon period or the early Norman.

Happily, everyone can agree that the 14th century saw important additions. Sometime after 1362, a group of four benefactors seem to have come together to build the bellcote, the north aisle, the chantry and perhaps the porch. Ironically these are the four areas of the church most criticised by modern commentators.

"Every part seems disproportionate to the rest," is Adrian S Pye's verdict published in *Parish Churches of East Norfolk*.

"The chantry chapel built on in the 14th century to the north side of the elegant chancel is a curious structure which does not marry well with the rest of the building," says online church expert Simon Knott.

More kindly, Mortlock & Roberts, describe the whole church as "small but tall for its size".

There were two further restorations in the 19th century, but very unusually for a medieval church, another followed in the 21st century. The new £435 000 community room – faced in Norfolk flint – was opened by the Bishop of Norwich in 2012.

Hellesdon Mill

Most mills perished to fire, but not Hellesdon's. Unlikely as it may seem, its demise was due to David Lloyd George's promise to build "homes fit for heroes" after the First World War. Norwich City Council was particularly inspired by the Prime Minister's words and bought the mill specifically to dismantle it.

So today all that remains are the brick foundations across the river – usually inaccessible behind a locked gate. But on the Hellesdon bank, stylish granary and malthouse buildings have made it through the dark decades between abandonment and restoration. They were converted into flats in the early years of this century.

The mill itself had been a substantial building. Of course it had been through many incarnations, but the version the city council raided was four storeys high with 66 windows on one side alone. Over the years the mill appears to have been used for everything from fulling (a stage in cloth-making) to grinding corn and producing linseed oil.

Hellesdon Mill: the surviving buildings

Hellesdon Hospital

It began life as Norwich City Asylum, later became known as Norwich City Mental Hospital and is now simply Hellesdon Hospital. But whatever the name, the core task of this

Hellesdon Hospital in the foreground with the river in the distance

huge institution has remained the same – helping to treat people who suffer from mental illness.

Space has never been an issue on this vast site between Drayton High Road and the Hellesdon Low Road. There was plenty of room for the first dormitories in the late 1870s: plenty of room too for the coach house, the stables and the staff cottages. At that time the hospital also owned a farm beyond Low Road where as many as 15 or 20 patients worked. According to one hospital history, they were rewarded with an ounce of tobacco twice a week.

Just architecturally, Hellesdon Hospital can tell you an awful lot about the changes in mental health treatment since the early days. The 50-acre site is still dominated by the ward buildings – testimony to the days when dormitories ruled. Just before the Second World War there were 750 in-patients. Today the number is far, far fewer.

It's not that people don't suffer from the same problems, just that today the vast majority are helped in their own homes.

"When you look at the history books you realise how much has changed," Estates Information Manager John Downes told me.

"Now we provide single bedrooms with *en suite* facilities and there has to be a certain number of square metres for each individual patient too. When we build these days, we're effectively building small hotel blocks."

Today the hospital is a big employer. The Norwich and Suffolk NHS Foundation Trust has its HQ here and many of its staff are based on site. They run everything from dementia wards to an Alcohol and Drugs Service. Over the decades Hellesdon Hospital has become a major part of Hellesdon life.

Hellesdon Station

The building has long gone, but the implications of Hellesdon Station are still with us. Hellesdon had been a quiet hamlet until the arrival of the new Midland & Great Northern railway line in 1882. Once connected to the city it grew quickly.

Hellesdon Station: long-gone

Hellesdon was the first stop on a line which started at City Station Norwich and continued north to Melton Constable. As well as the station building, old maps show a signal box, sidings and cattle pens.

The line's golden years were probably between the wars. Certainly the rise of the motor car after the Second World War proved to be its undoing. Hellesdon Station closed in 1952, seven years earlier than the other stations.

The station building survived for a little longer, becoming a well-used church hall until it was demolished in the early 1960s.

Today all that remains at Hellesdon are parts of the platform. But strip back the foliage in your mind and it's easy to imagine the sights and the sounds of steam.

To find the station site, cross Hellesdon Road next to the river, heading away from Norwich. Ignore the signs telling you to turn left for Marriotts Way and cross straight over on to a narrow footpath. The M&GN archaeology is on your left-hand side.

Briar Chemicals

In the middle of suburbia, a giant chemical complex. This collection of factories started life in 1955 when London-based May & Baker was looking to expand. Its staff came across a 100-odd acre area of farmland in Hellesdon and decided to take the plunge.

Sixty years later they're still going strong, even if Hellesdon residents with long memories can remember a number of different name plates on the gates. After May & Baker it was Rhone Poulenc then Aventis CropScience, then Bayer CropScience. It's been Briar Chemicals – an independent company owned by German investors – since 2012. In recent years they've concentrated on making "intermediates" – in other words chemicals which other companies use to make products for the market place.

"It's been tougher since the site has been run as an independent company," says site manager Tim Green.

An aerial shot of the Briar Chemicals site in 1976

"But we're doing well and we're investing. We've recently spent £5million improving the on-site treatment here."

The factory occupies a big site from Sweetbriar Road in the east to Hellesdon Road in the west. Hellesdon Hall Road is the northern boundary, Marriotts Way lies to the south. Security is tight of course. But partially as a result, wildlife flourishes. Mr Green says the lack of public access means that rare moths and orchids thrive here.

In the past this place has provided employment for more than 1000 people. These days it's about 230 plus an average of 40 contractors.

ARCHIVE: *The May & Baker Scandal*

In the mid-1980s the May & Baker chemical factory in Hellesdon was at the centre of a pollution scandal – one of the most serious Norwich has ever seen.

It barely gets a mention on the internet, but as ever the Norfolk Record Office fills in the gaps, with its bulging file of newspaper articles from the *Eastern Daily Press* and news scripts from BBC Radio Norfolk.

Thanks to the tenacity of Friends of the Earth, it became clear that the May & Baker factory had been polluting the aquifers beneath its site for years. Much of the pollution had travelled by pipe and by sewer to the Whitlingham treatment works – meaning that the River Yare was badly affected. Elsewhere it had infected some boreholes at the Anglian Water works at nearby Heigham.

The first revelation in the NRO file comes in November 1985. Friends of the Earth analysed eels caught in the Yare and discovered they were contaminated with mercury. It was a "smoking gun".

By December the group was claiming that a plan to build more storage tanks at the waterworks had been abandoned because of a "chemical cocktail" seeping into the groundwater.

In January 1986 the city council called a conference in an attempt to bang heads together, but by March the case was a national *cause célèbre*. The *Eastern Evening News* looked back to November and argued that "since then a blaze of rumour, misunderstanding and accusation has flared, unquenched by meaningless reassurances from the two organisations most closely involved – Anglian Water and May & Baker."

In the words of a government minister at the time, this pollution "threatened but did not reach" the city's water supply. But as a result Anglian Water fast tracked existing plans for a new pipeline. Water was now taken from the Wensum upriver at Costessey, rather than at Heigham.

Both companies started to act – and they did so much more publicly than they had done in the past. Drains were improved, dykes were lined, contaminated top soil was removed.

A generation later, it seems extraordinary that while the authorities had known there was a problem since the early 1980s, nothing was made public until 1985/6.

And today? Today, the site is owned by Briar Chemicals. Its site manager Tim Green acknowledged the mistakes of a previous generation but added: "Practices are very different now. We work very closely with the Environment Agency".

St Paul's Church

Alfred Cossey

St Paul's Church

St Paul's is some distance from the Wensum and so doesn't really belong in a book called Riverside Norwich. But this survivor does illustrate how Hellesdon has changed over the years.

As the housing estates spread eastwards after the Second World War, St Mary's church was no longer close enough for many or big enough for all. The parish needed a so-called daughter church. But with money and raw materials equally short, a Nissen Hut – albeit a Nissen Hut dignified with a brick façade - was the best that they could do.

"It's too hot in the summer and it's too cold in the winter and it always has been" said long-time parishioner Alfred Cossey.

"But I would be very sad to see this place pulled down. There again that's probably because my wife Anne and I were married here in 1951."

"I've got a great love for both churches," he added. "St Mary's offers a traditional service whereas St Paul's is more modern." And then, with a nod at the drum kit in the corner he adds, "I enjoy a band rather than an organ."

More than sixty years on this church and this congregation seem as vibrant as ever.

The Marl Pit Area

Norwich's housing stock suffered terribly during the Second World War. More than 3000 properties suffered bomb damage of which 2000 were beyond repair. One solution – the famous "pre-fabs" houses built mostly on green-field sites. And so it was that a triangle of land between Dereham Road and the River Wensum started to become the Marl Pit estate. A total of 228 homes on streets like Bates Road and Gentry Road were meant to be a short-term solution. Ultimately they survived for a generation, disappearing as recently as 1968.

The pre-fabs were replaced by a mixture of flats and houses that now provide more solid homes for hundreds of people. Those on Hellesdon Road itself have great views across the river.

Marl is a mixture of lime and clay which was widely used in the 18th and 19th centuries to improve farming land. Further down the Wensum at Whitlingham it was dug out in vast quantities and shipped by wherry.

The pit here was on the west side of Marl Pit lane – roughly where White Rose Close lies today or perhaps the playing fields behind.

The Marlpit pub

St Michael's foundation stone: dragged from the skip

The Marl Pit pub closed down in May 2014, but should re-open in 2016 after a spirited campaign by locals. You might imagine that this elegant building had been a licensed premises since Victorian times. In reality it was a farm until at least 1937 and perhaps until after the Second World War. Take another look at the outbuildings and the extensive grounds and it begins to make sense.

And finally in Marl Pit, it's worth mentioning a church which used to sit opposite the pub. Like St Paul's (see separate entry), St Michael's in the Marl Pit was a daughter church of St Mary's. Like St Paul's it was built as a response to a huge increase in the population after the war.

"There were a lot of young people who went to Sunday School in the old railway station building in Hellesdon in the 1950s," explained long-time parishioner Ginny Smith.

"But British Rail wanted to pull that building down. And that was when we decided that we wanted to build a church and a community hall here on the Marl Pit."

The congregation pretty much built it with their bare hands, or, as the official record has it, "with a minimum of professional help". Designed more as a community hall, it had a sanctuary which could be screened off when services were not being held. It was dedicated by the Bishop of Norwich in 1965.

Later another community centre was built on the opposite side of the road. At St Michael's, vicars came and went, the congregation dwindled and the building began to show its age. Renovation work would have been too expensive and it was decided demolition was the only option. In 2011 new houses went up in its place.

Now only the foundation stone survives – and even that was a close call. "We had to drag it out of the skip ourselves," said Mrs Smith. "But the builders were happy to include it within the development once we'd brought it to their attention."

"We built that church with our own hands, so yes, to see it fall into disrepair after so many happy years was very, very sad."

Canoeing The Wensum *Hellesdon to Heigham*

Distance: 2 miles return trip

Launching a canoe is easy from the car park on Hellesdon Mill Lane. From there the river flows south and you shoot Hellesdon Bridge and the Marriotts Way bridge in quick succession. Now it turns east and you'll make out Briar Chemicals to the left while the Marl Pit estate emerges on the right. The Wensum then does one of its disappearing acts to all but us river-users. You paddle behind the newly-listed Gatehouse pub and out of sight past allotments to Sweet Briar bridge carrying the outer ring road. The under-rated Sweet Briar Road meadows take over to the left with a foot bridge giving walkers access from Sycamore Crescent. Now the Heigham Waterworks dominate on the right bank. You're soon at Mile Cross bridge and then the Gibraltar Gardens pub. After a drink there, turn around and head for home.

The footbridge from Sycamore Crescent

Chapter 6 Mile Cross to Oak Street

Riverside views from the Clickers Road development

This is the transitional chapter, it starts in suburbia and ends in the city. And annoyingly from my point of view, the area to the north of the Wensum from Drayton Road to Oak Street doesn't have an over-arching name. It's part Mile Cross, part North City and part Coslany.

As ever it's simpler down on the river. The Wensum leaves Hellesdon behind as it flows under the Sweet Briar bridge on Norwich's outer ring road. On the south bank we're then in Heigham, where the water treatment works dominate the landscape. On the north bank the Sweet Briar Road meadows provide a welcome "green lung" between Marriotts Way and the river.

Mile Cross Bridge is the next landmark. A city council depot and refuse tip share the riverside with a travellers' site. Then we find another well-used green space, Anderson's Meadow. Now the river turns south, soon rubbing up against Wensum Park and then St Martin's Road. Modern flats and houses make the most of the location and it's great to see so many canoes semi-camouflaged within private gardens.

And then to Oak Street. Remember that in the old days, living near the river meant disease and the risk of flooding. Only the poorest dwelt close to the Wensum and they lived cheek by jowl with each other too. The yards and terraces here were among the most god-forsaken slums in all of Norwich. Overlooked and under-appreciated, this part of the city once teemed with life.

Sweet Briar Bridge

This elegant two-span bridge was built in the 1930s as one of the final pieces in the jigsaw of the outer ring road. As a driver you're hard pushed to notice it. As a canoeist heading downstream it's a suitably grand start to the river's city life.

Mile Cross Bridge

Indisputably the ugliest bridge across the Wensum, The Mile Cross Bridge dates back to the early 1920s. It was built as part of an unemployment relief project and helped serve the new council estates which were springing up to the north of the river. Reinforced concrete was then the material of the future. Functional and durable, yes. Pretty, no.

Dolphin Bridge

This one also gets a mention in the Heigham chapter. It was built as a pedestrian bridge in 1909 to replace the Dolphin Ferry. Many at the time felt it should have been built for cars too. Originally it was longer, allowing people to cross the old Midland & Great Northern railway line. Marriotts Way now runs in the railway's place.

From top:
Sweet Briar Bridge
Mile Cross Bridge
Dolphin Bridge

From top:
Marriotts Way Bridge
St Crispin's Bridge

Marriotts Way Bridge

The M&GN line used to cross the Wensum here via an A-frame bridge not dissimilar to the one still in place at Drayton. A wooden bridge was installed in 1986 and was replaced with this more elaborate metal and concrete creation in 2002. It was designed by artist Les Bicknell.

"I went and sat around the old bridge just about every day for two months to chat to the people who used it," he told me. "I spoke to fishermen, runners, the kids who were bunking off school, everyone. And all that text that you see on the steps of the bridge came from them."

St Crispin's Road Bridges

Again as a motorist you barely notice, but the inner ring road crosses the Wensum via two bridges. Those heading towards Grapes Hill travel across an iron bridge made in 1882 by the local foundry – Barnard, Bishop & Barnard. Drivers heading east are on the much more straightforward concrete bridge built when the inner ring road was created in 1972.

Sweet Briar Road Meadows

Technically they are unimproved wet meadows made up of a mixture of marshy grassland and tall fen. Practically they provide a great place to walk the dog and taste the countryside. According to English Nature, the 22-acre Site of Special Scientific Interest is something of a rarity. Elsewhere, drainage and farming improvements have often changed this sort of river valley habitat.

Sweet Briar's SSSI

ARCHIVE: *The Norwich River*

Rivers meant more in the old days, so much so, that each short stretch had its own name. Along navigable stretches of the Yare for example, these so-called reaches remain well-known – at least to sailors and rowers. But up here on the Wensum it was a surprise to discover a similar pattern. The secrets are to be found in a bulky but ancient document in the Norfolk Record Office entitled "The Norwich River from Hellesdon Bridge to the New Mills" from 1767. Each leaf of this book has long since become detached from the remains of its spine. And sticky burnt patches on the calfskin-covered strawboard show it only just survived the disastrous Norwich Central Library fire of 1994.

But the pages tell a story. A small tight meander close to Heigham Water treatment works is revealed (in swirling faded-brown ink) to be Horse Shoe Reach. The long straight stretch next to Briar Chemicals is Washers Reach. Three Tree Reach and Sullers Hole Reach approximate to the Wensum Park stretch, while Bleach Reach and Dam Reach follow in quick succession as the river heads down to what is now the inner ring road. Washers Reach and Bleach Reach undoubtedly give us clues as to how the river was used 250 years ago. Together they offer an opaque but tantalising window into a world which has long-since disappeared.

The Mile Cross Estate

With 21st century eyes it is so difficult to see this development as it would have appeared to its first residents. Don't get me wrong, the big houses and wide boulevards still make it a cut above most estates. But in the 1920s this really would have felt like the promised land. And that's why I include it, even though much of it is some distance north of the river.

Mile Cross: tree-lined avenues and houses fit for heroes

First, we forget how grim life was for the majority in the immediate aftermath of the First World War. There was mass unemployment and occasionally mass unrest – riots and looting on the streets of Norwich in December 1920 for example. Inevitably it took time to build the famous "homes fit for heroes", but one gets the feeling the authorities simply had no alternative, such was the anger.

Second, the tenants were swapping tiny, damp, overcrowded slums with shared outside loos for spacious three-bedroomed houses with indoor bathrooms – a real rarity in that era.

Mile Cross was one of four council estates planned for Norwich at this time. The others were at Earlham, around Angel Road and Harford Hall. Mile Cross was planned along the lines of a garden suburb and it was the first such council estate in the country. After the horrors of the First World War, these were truly homes fit for heroes.

PEOPLE: *Stuart McPherson*

Like many a council estate in many a city, Mile Cross has felt itself to be underappreciated over the years. So, in this decade and on this estate, how best to lift the mood? Step forward photographer Stuart McPherson. Stuart grew up on Drayton Road and now lives with his family just around the corner on Pinder Road. He knows every nook and cranny of the estate. And in 2015 his solution to the Mile Cross image problem was to create new images of Mile Cross – photos showcased on the flickr website.

Armed with a Canon EOS 5D, he has that enviable ability of making you see familiar places with a fresh eye. The original design principles of the garden suburb come shining through. The decades get stripped away and we see those wide streets, the elegant library and its thriving community centres for what they really are.

"It was the first housing estate in Norwich and I love its history," he told me.

"I love the fact that it was built by soldiers returning from the First World War. If you take time to look at the architecture, you'll see that it is beautiful. But people often don't realise what they've got on their own doorstep."

Stuart clearly does. Each of the photos comes complete with a story or a memory from his childhood. Thousands have looked at them, many have left comments of their own.

Those planners, those returning soldiers too, would surely approve.

Go to https://www.flickr.com/photos/stumcp/albums and look for Mile Cross.

The Edwards & Holmes Shoe Factory

So how many of the residents in the smart town houses of Bootbinders Road, Finishers Road and Clickers Road know why their streets are so named? This photo provides the answer. The massive Edwards & Holmes shoe factory dominated this stretch of the Wensum for 90 years until its demolition in 2002. Edwards & Holmes was one of a number of big names in an industry which employed thousands in Norwich throughout the 19th and 20th centuries. We'll find other former factories as we head south.

Edwards & Holmes shoe factory

Edwards & Holmes had started life in a cramped cottage in the city centre but quickly outgrew both that and a building in Esdelle Street. This factory was their third, and despite the best efforts of the 1912 floods, it was state-of-the-art when it opened for business in 1913. Hundreds of thousands of shoes were manufactured here. Many were exported.

Confusingly called the "Esdelle Works" in memory of their earlier factory, the building was totally destroyed during the Baedeker Raids of April 1942. W L Sparks wrote a history of shoemaking in Norwich in 1949 when memories were still fresh:

"Everything was destroyed, stock, fixtures and records, lasts and patterns, all were reduced to ashes in the fire caused by the incendiary bombs."

It was quickly rebuilt after the war and thrived right through until the 1980s when competition from cheaper-made foreign shoes started to have an impact. Facing financial difficulties, the company was taken over in 1987. I understand it closed down in the early 1990s.

And what did the clickers and finishers do? Clickers cut the leather uppers, while finishers were involved in the last stage of the process, tidying the sole and making the shoe waterproof.

PEOPLE: *Dick Lubbuck*

Dick Lubbuck is one of the few people left who can remember the first incarnation of the Edwards & Holmes factory next to the Wensum – the building that was bombed in 1942.

He started work in the pattern-making department in 1939. Aged just 14, they paid him 9 shillings a week. And apart from a stint in the Royal Navy from 1943 to 1946, he worked there all his life, returning to a new building which rose from the ashes of the old one:

"By 1947–8 the whole factory was completely finished," he remembers. "The machine room was at one end near Wensum Park and the clicking room and the pattern-making room and the leather room were at the other end."

He spent most of his time in the pattern-making department at a time when Edwards & Holmes was a big name – so much so that it made shoes for the Queen. Mr Lubbuck was responsible for drawing up the patterns for four pairs – HM took size 5½B, he recalls.

He estimates that there were probably 300 or 400 employees when he first started, far fewer towards the end. He retired in 1990 after completing a remarkable 50 years with one company on one site.

And in case any modern residents of Clickers Road wonder, yes he did time as a clicker: qualified to cut the leather and defined by the noise the special knives made. Calf, suede and sheepskin, he's cut them all. Two factories, one bombing and one new housing estate, he's seen it all too.

Wensum Park

It was once a hive of industry, later became a rubbish dump and is now a peaceful riverside refuge. The modern Wensum Park was created during the 1920s by Captain Sandys-Winsch as part of a scheme to provide useful work for the unemployed people of Norwich.

According to the Captain's biographer A P Anderson, the land was bought by the city council as early as 1907. Some progress on building a swimming pool and a children's pool

Wensum Park: the Captain's finest work

was made the following year but ground to a halt in 1910. It then became a semi-official rubbish tip until work was finally completed in 1921.

Anderson describes it as the most natural of the Captain's four Norwich parks – the others being Eaton, Waterloo and Heigham.

"It is the only one of the four parks to adjoin either of the two Norwich rivers and this fact gives the Park its character. The site slopes from the formalities of the main entrance, from where fine views across the river can be gained, down to the dyke, which running from the river and parallel to it was the site of a water garden, Sandys-Winsch at his most imaginative."

The City Wall

Norwich used to be a walled city and here, as St Martin's Road turns into Oak Street, we enter what used to be the inner sanctum. Look left along Bakers Road and the remains of the wall are there for all to see. Look down as well. The narrow bed of flints amid the grass verge shows where the wall continued. Look right and you will see No 167 Oak Street. This was once the Dun Cow pub. Here, the city wall was also the pub wall and a substantial chunk remains in the building's cellar.

Now take a short diversion down the alley for more remains, this time of a so-called mural tower. The river used to be wider and include many channels here. One theory is that the

The remains of a mural tower

City wall, city terraces

tower marked the Wensum's banks in those wilder days. From Baker Street the wall runs across St Augustine's Street to give Magpie Road its shape. From there it shadows Bull Close Road before heading south to hit the river opposite Norwich Crown Court.

On the Heigham side of the river the wall continued slightly downstream - presumably because this area was very marshy – before marching along Barn Road towards Grapes Hill.

Oak Street itself was once protected by St Martin's Gate, one of 13 entrances into Norwich which could be closed every evening and during times of conflict.

The wall as a whole dates back to the 13th and 14th centuries and was called into action on many occasions. It was last barricaded during the Civil War. But during the following century the gates and the walls began to be seen as an inconvenience. According to one Victorian writer St Martin's Gate was dismantled in 1808.

The Great Hall

Oak Street is a commercial street, a place where things are made, bought and sold. Today the wares include everything from sheds to windscreens, new motorbikes to old cars.

The Great Hall: Oak Street's hidden gem

But among the modern shop fronts and older reclamation yards lies evidence of a grander commercial past, a 15th century building known simply as The Great Hall.

It's one of the many historical wonders of Norwich that such stylish buildings should survive in the most unlikely of locations. Uproot the Great Hall to the city centre, open it to the public and we'd all pay good money to admire its mullioned windows and oriel archway. But as a private house in busy old Oak Street, relatively few people know it exists at all.

Architectural historians describe it as a "Hall House" – in other words a public hall complete with private living accommodation. And, as historian G N Barrett writes, it would have been built by a prosperous citizen when Oak Street was an integral part of Norwich's industrial suburb. Over the years it's been abandoned and rediscovered, bought, sold and redesigned. Today it is a private house owned and rented out by a modern merchant – Paul Clarke, whose Moonraker Motorcycles business is directly next door:

"I started as a neighbour and over the years I saw it in various states of disrepair according to which tenant was in it," he told me.

"And it often lay empty too, which obviously wasn't good for the building. So in 2009 I bought it. And since then I've restored it."

"I do love my history and what I love about the building is that you can look back and see all the other owners and their other occupations right across the centuries."

SS&E: a grand old shoe factory

Sexton Son & Everard

Oak Street was badly hit by the construction of the inner ring road in the early 1970s. The rise of the motor car meant the council had little alternative, but nothing destroys a sense of community quite like a dual-carriageway cutting your road in half.

Sextons had been founded in 1886 by Henry Sexton and his five sons. A disastrous fire at their premises on Fishergate in 1913 saw a new company Sexton Son & Everard rise from the ashes. They built a replacement factory at St Miles and added a bigger one – almost opposite – in 1921. The older factory was bombed during the war, meaning that the company needed every inch of the vast 90 000 square feet in the surviving building.

This grand old shoe factory is one of the first buildings you come to on the city side of Oak Street. Vast, sleek and much-admired when it was built in the 1920s, they made shoes here for decades.

The company called in the receivers in 1972. Its new owner, according to Nick Williams in his book *Norwich City of Industries* then made several hundred people redundant, making the announcement over the public address system. It finally closed in 1976.

Today, as St Mary's Works, the building is sub-let to many different companies.

New Mills

The building on the New Mills site today is neither new, nor a mill, nor plural come to think of it. But over the centuries, mills new and old have harnessed the power of the Wensum here and they've played a surprisingly pivotal role in Norwich's history.

Below : *New Mills: head of navigation*

Bottom: *The final navigable reach of the Wensum*

The date of the first mill is lost in antiquity. One could well have existed before the Norman Conquest. We think the "New" refers to mills built in about 1430 when they were used to grind corn.

These buildings were at the centre of a major row between the city fathers and the church authorities: the church (then – as now – a major landowner) claiming that the mill affected the flow of the river upstream at Heigham. Relations between church and city were troublesome throughout this period, but it's still surprising to learn that the precise amount of water flowing through a mill could provoke what historians call "Gladman's Insurrection" in 1443. As many as 3000 people effectively besieged Norwich's cathedral close, threatening to burn the priory and kill the monks. A noble called Gladman was alleged to have imitated the king, prompting accusations of treason. Ultimately the real king had to get involved and it was four years before the city was forgiven.

By the 16th century New Mills was also being used as a source of drinking water, with supplies being pumped towards the city centre. Private houses could now pay to have water on tap – even if the quality would be questionable for centuries. By the 17th century more formal "waterworks" are mentioned while it was clear that the power of the water was still being used to help fullers to clean cloth and millers to grind corn.

Then in 1766 the New Mills was besieged by a mob wanting fairer prices for food. This food riot was one of a number to erupt across the country at this time. The mill itself seems to have survived but a large malthouse was set on fire.

The 19th century saw increasing concern over the quality of the water entering the waterworks. With untold factories and privies upstream, the New Mills was fighting an unequal battle and it was no surprise when a new waterworks was built at Heigham – a good mile upstream. The last miller left a few years later and the mill buildings were finally pulled down in 1893. What we see now is a Victorian pneumatic ejection sewage pump put out of its misery in 1973, together with some still-useful sluices. Crucially it remains the head of navigation for boats on the Wensum. (Canoeists of course can resort to a bit of portage.)

So what should we do with it now? True, the only other such sewage pump is to be found at the Houses of Parliament (insert your own metaphor here). But in reality New Mills is a modest building on an unattractive bridge without a hope of finding a useful purpose. Is it time to knock it down?

The old Anchor Brewery

Anchor Brewery

The best barley in the world was grown in the fields of Norfolk, wrote the mid-20th century writer James Wentworth Day. And the water percolating up through a chalky subsoil wasn't bad either. All the ingredients, he argued, for a thriving brewing industry. The old Anchor Brewery, hard up against the Wensum in the Coslany area of Norwich, is the first of three we will encounter on our journey down the river.

Founded by Richard Bullard and James Watts in 1837, the brewery expanded throughout the 19th century, covering two acres at its height. Bullard's son Harry took over in 1864 and later sank an artesian well on the site to ensure clean water.

Brewery historian Andrew P Davison says that by the turn of the century the company owned 280 pubs, leased another 161 and owned seven malthouses.

Like the city's other breweries, Bullards fell victim to a rash of greedy takeovers in the decades after the Second World War. The factory closed in 1968. The 120-feet high chimney, which can be seen in every old photo of this part of Norwich, clung on until 1982.

Crucially, enough buildings survived to be converted into flats within the Anchor housing development. So while this part of Norwich is now resolutely residential, it still feels as if it hasn't quite lost its brewing soul. But that distinctive, hoppy aroma has gone forever.

The Bike Ride *Mile Cross*

Distance: 2 miles

From the car park at Sloughbottom Park take the cycle path signposted to Hellesdon Hall Road and head up to Sweet Briar Road. Turn right, heading towards the Asda junction where you'll see a surviving boundary cross, marking the old border between city and county.

Keep on the ring road and stop for drinks at The Whiffler – the pub of choice for Mile Cross residents. (And if you want to know what a whiffler was, find the relevant info board in the pub.)

Then take the steep cycle path directly opposite the pub and turn right on to Bowers Avenue, home of the tall Markham, Aylmer and Seaman tower blocks. Continue along Bowers Avenue then take a sharp right down Galley Hill to the site of the old Galley Hill pub, now a hair and beauty salon.

Turn left on to Drayton Road and then first right on to Valpy Avenue which has great views from the allotments across the Wensum valley. Take a footpath on the right which returns to Sloughbottom Park. From here you can head into the city centre along Marriotts Way or return to the car park.

Sloughbottom Park: for all ages

Chapter 7 Heigham

Heigham started off as a medieval hamlet close to, but separate from Norwich. It had a church and was later famous for its Bishop's Palace and a venerable old pub called the Gibraltar Gardens.

The Wensum was Heigham's northern boundary and it would have felt much more like a boundary in those early days. There were no bridges between the city and Hellesdon until the 20th century, so local people had to rely on a "carnser" (the Norfolk word for a causeway) and a ferry.

All that started to change in the 19th century when Norwich expanded in Heigham's direction. A substantial island within the Wensum was drained to become the site of City Station. Then a massive waterworks was built on the site of the old common.

Technically the parish spread south towards Eaton. And during the 19th century the fields belonging to landlords like Clement William Unthank were quickly colonised by smart terraced housing. The population leapt from 5000 in 1821 to 24 000 in 1881. Heigham split in two. South Heigham was the smart new suburb – what we now call the Golden Triangle. North Heigham was its more industrial neighbour.

This compact, working class community had the heart ripped out during two nights in the spring of 1942. Large parts of Norwich suffered terribly during Hitler's Baedeker raids on April 27th and April 29th, but you could argue that Heigham suffered most of all.

Opposite: *The Wensum seen from behind Sycamore Crescent*

Finally a word on pronunciation. I've heard three different versions. "Haaam" from the real old school; "Hey-am" from their sons and daughters and finally "High-am" from us outsiders. Take your pick.

St Bartholomew's Church

At first sight it's like dozens of other urban parks in Norwich. But in the middle there's something much more incongruous: a 15th century church tower without a church.

That's because this park was once a graveyard. And the tower belonged to the medieval St Bartholomew's. All that changed on April 29th 1942 – the night of the second of the Baedeker raids. The church was blown to smithereens, the bells came crashing down, the font was split into pieces and just about all of the interior timberwork went up in smoke.

St Bartholomew's: you feel the absence of a church

A rector, visiting a week later, found parts of the church still smouldering. He reported how a safe containing parish registers had survived the blast, only for some of the papers to instantly combust on exposure to the air. Photos taken at the time show that some walls did survive, but there never seems to have been any question of a rebuild. Instead the parishioners moved to an old Methodist chapel nearby. Everything but the tower was deemed unsafe and demolished in 1953.

St Bartholomew's had been the parish church for Heigham for centuries. It was probably most famous as the church where the exiled bishop Joseph Hall had preached during the Civil War. The church had fallen on hard times during the Victorian era, but was restored and extended during the 1870s.

Today its tower is a poignant reminder of the bombings. Albeit a low-key, all-but-forgotten reminder in an often over-looked part of Norwich.

Top: *Gibraltar Gardens*

Above: *The Dolphin Inn: now a chiropractors*

Gibraltar Gardens

The Gibraltar Gardens is the only pub along the River Wensum where the thirsty canoeist can be on the river bank one minute and at the bar the next. As such it has a lot going for it, although staff have occasionally looked askance at the (small) puddles I have brought in with me.

Now Grade II listed, parts of the building date back to the 15th century even if its present name probably came along a lot later. One local historian connects it to the capture of Gibraltar by the British in 1704. Who was responsible he asks? A Norfolkman, the delightfully-named Admiral Sir Cloudsley Shovell.

The Dolphin Inn

The Dolphin Inn and the Gibraltar Gardens are the grand old men of Heigham, with almost a thousand years of history between them. But while the Gibraltar has generally kept its nose clean, The Dolphin has had a tougher time.

Built of knapped flint and stone towards the end of the 16th century, it first came to prominence about 50 years later when it became the home of Joseph Hall – the bishop ejected from his own cathedral during the Civil War. It was here – in semi-exile – that Hall wrote many of his learned works on Christian meditation.

According to the norfolkpubs website, it had changed from being called "Bishop Hall's Palace" to The Dolphin, perhaps by 1752 and certainly by 1794. Landlords quickly started to make the most of its riverside location, adding swimming baths by the middle of the 19th century. And before the Dolphin Bridge was added in 1909, there was a ferry too.

Both the pub and the baths received a direct hit on the first night of the Baedeker bombings. The brewers Steward & Patteson had it rebuilt by 1960 before it succumbed to our declining need for pubs in 1999. It is currently the home of the Norwich Chiropractic Centre.

Finally some inconvenient facts. First, it was never officially a palace despite the nearby Old Palace Road. Second, Bishop Hall's biographer Frank Livingstone Huntley thinks it's more likely that Hall lived in a more modest house on the opposite side of Old Palace Road. But hey, let's not let either get in the way of a good story.

PEOPLE: *Bishop Joseph Hall*

As well-known in his day as the poet John Milton and the Norwich author Sir Thomas Browne, Bishop Joseph Hall is all-but forgotten in the 21st century. He wasn't from Norwich and he arrived here almost by accident, but I'd argue he's still worth a statue in what used to be St Bartholomew's graveyard.

He was one of the most learned men of his day. He preached to King James I, had high-profile rows with Milton and was regarded as "our English Seneca" – a reference to one of Rome's most famous philosophers. He was also a man who sought peace and compromise amidst the poisonous religious atmosphere of 17th century England.

He was promoted to Bishop of Norwich in 1641 by Charles I, brought in to try to placate the amazing number of religious minorities in the city at the time.

But later that same year Hall was one of 12 bishops to be impeached by Parliament. And as widespread discord turned to all-out civil war he spent several months locked up in the Tower of London, accused of high treason. He eventually made it to his diocese and his cathedral, but less than a year later he was evicted by Parliamentary commissioners.

And then he turned to unfashionable, marshy Heigham. What was later known as The Dolphin Inn apparently became his home, his place of exile. As his biographer Frank Livingstone Huntley makes clear, he still regarded himself as Bishop of Norwich, but he had neither diocese nor cathedral. Indeed he is one of our best eye-witnesses for the furious desecration of Norwich Cathedral at the hands of Parliamentary forces:

"What clattering of glasses, what beating down of walls, what tearing up of monuments, what pulling down of seats, what wrestling out of irons and brass from the windows and graves, what defacing of arms, what demolishing of curious stonework…

"What tooting and piping upon the destroyed organ-pipes, what a hideous triumph on the market day before all the country, when, in a kind of sacrilegious and profane procession, all the organ-pipes, vestments, both copes and surplices together with the leaden cross… were carried to the fire in the public market place; a lewd wretch walking before the train in his cope trailing in the dirt…"

The Bishop died in 1656 and was buried at St Bartholomew's. A man, according to one of his contemporaries, "of singular humility, patience and pietie".

He finally returned to the cathedral in 1975 when his remains were reinterred in a corner of its cloister garth after a ceremony conducted by his successor. After more than 300 years, the banishment of Bishop Hall was finally over.

The Swimming Baths Of Heigham

I grew up in the age of the leisure centre. For me, swimming pools were indoor, heated and chlorinated. Previous generations had it much colder.

Many learnt to swim in outdoor pools built next to and within the river itself. And the curiosity in Norwich was that there were two of these "river baths" within half a mile of each other in Heigham, together with a rare indoor pool.

It's hard to explain exactly how the outdoor ones worked. There would normally be some sort of underwater concrete tank within the river, with rudimentary changing cubicles at the water's edge. Other smaller baths were sometimes cut into the bank itself.

So starting up river, **Swan Baths** comes first. This indoor pool was an offshoot of the Swan Laundry built by the Norwich Steam Laundry and Baths Company in the 1870s , with the steam used to heat the pool. It inspired 13 men to set up the Swan Amateur Swimming Club – one of the earliest such clubs in the country. The *Eastern Daily Press* columnist Jonathan Mardle was taught there in the early years of the 20th century by a man nicknamed "Strawberry Nose".

"I went very slowly, one at a time down the step that led into the shallow end, gasping as the cold water rose first to my knees, then to my thighs, then to my waist... when I had a little recovered, I slipped the canvas loop under my arms, and Strawberry Nose dangled me from the end of a bamboo pole as if I were a decidedly incompetent fish that he had caught."

Left to right:

The dapper young men of Swan Baths...

...on the site of Old Laundry Court

Left to right:

Swimming lessons at one of the baths along the Wensum

Members of the Swan Swimming Club at The Eagle Baths

The pool closed in 1933 but the Swan swimming club was just getting into its stride. It started to hold lessons and galas at other pools and by 1980 it had approximately 1600 members with classes across the Norwich area. It continues to thrive to this day.

The Swan Laundry – without a pool – continued until 1979 and the building, Swan House, was demolished in roughly 2000. Today the smart town houses of Old Laundry Court occupy the same site.

The Eagle Baths – on the site of the present Eagle Canoe Club – lay only a few hundred yards downriver from the Swan. When it opened in 1906 it was hailed as "one of the finest open-air baths in the Eastern Counties". There were actually two baths, a large one within the main river for the men and a smaller one cut into the bank for women.

The Norwich Penguins Swimming Club (also still in existence) ran its club nights here from 1934 and, according to its own history, persuaded the city council to build a five metre diving platform on the far bank. We think these baths closed in the 1950s.

Yet a few hundred yards further downriver lay **The Dolphin Baths** which date back to at least the mid-19th century. The Norwich historian Walter Rye, writing in 1917, described it as:

"Once a most -pleasant swimming bathing-place, with clear water and a gravel bottom, and a little island for a half-way house for nervous swimmers."

A Professor James Carey was in charge around the turn of the century. Famous for having saved 25 people from drowning, he went on to run a boat-letting business alongside The Dolphin. The baths were well used by the Swan Swimming Club after their own indoor pool closed in the 1930s. Like the pub, these baths were bombed during the Second World War.

PEOPLE: *Bridget & Richard Belson*

Bridget Belson's first experience of swimming was an eight year old at the outdoor Lakenham Baths in the years after the Second World War. She hated it.

"The bottom was so slippery that it was impossible to stand up – and that made it very difficult to stay upright when you were learning," she remembers with a smile more than 65 years later.

But she stuck with it and would soon grow to love the sport. After joining the Norwich Swan Swimming Club in 1952, she went on to become a county champion in both swimming and diving. By that stage the Swan was holding lessons at pools across the city. She met her future husband Richard Belson at the recently-opened St Augustine's Pool in 1961 and the couple later went on to serve as chairman and secretary for many years.

"What we always liked about the club was that it was fun and it was competitive, but the competition wasn't the be-all and end-all," she said. "If the children wanted to give up on the competitive side we would try to channel them into life saving or water polo."

"There was a good social side too," added Richard. "And we always encouraged the older kids to look after the younger ones. We gave them the responsibility and they always rose to the occasion."

These days Bridget is the club archivist. The Swan, it transpires, was one of the first swimming clubs in the country, so it's quite a job. And Bridget has several files with cuttings, photographs and gala programmes that span the decades.

The Swan Laundry might be long gone, but the swimming club it helped inspire, is still very much alive.

Heigham Water Treatment Works

If you fill up your kettle or brush your teeth in Norwich, you'll be using Wensum water. To be more precise, it's water which leaves the Wensum at Costessey, travels four miles down a 32" pipe under Marriotts Way and sits ready and waiting in a Victorian reservoir at Heigham.

Here on a vast site with a long history, the clever stuff happens. Anglian Water takes the raw river water and turns it into something "wholesome and safe". We take it for granted, but of course life wasn't always this simple.

Before 1850, drinking most water in Norwich was a hazardous activity. True, supplies were drawn off the Wensum at New Mills and pumped to a reservoir on the site of what is now Chapelfield Gardens. But it wasn't treated and consequently it wasn't healthy. Looking back in 1919, one journalist on the *Eastern Daily Press* remembered those days with horror:

"What the citizens had to drink in those days must have been appalling, for Chapel Field was anything but the flowery and salubrious promenade it has since become.

"How the citizens of those days suffered for their neglect of so vital a matter as purity of the water can only be surmised. What we do know for sure is that Norwich is no longer infamous for the prevalence of calcareous diseases, and that the race of pock-marked people familiar to the memory of every man past middle-age seems utterly to have disappeared."

A national cholera epidemic during 1848 and 1849 had prompted much soul-searching in Britain. Norwich had escaped relatively lightly, but everyone knew how poor the city's facilities were. Away from the Chapelfield reservoir, many relied on parish pumps in city graveyards. Here the water could be truly vile, contaminated as it often was by recently buried bodies.

In this climate, the government was happy to see either councils or private companies get involved. Norwich went down the private route. On June 6th 1850, The City of Norwich Waterworks Act allowed 12 Norwich men to set up a treatment works at land "near Heigham Common". It would take a while but the city was on its way to getting safe drinking water for good.

Lean over the substantial brick walls on Waterworks Road today and two tall buildings dominate the view. To the right, the Sultzer Engine Room, named after one of those first 12 men and dating back to 1858. It housed a massive beam engine – the power behind the pumps which would extract water from the Wensum. (The pipe from Costessey wouldn't arrive until much later.) The Sultzer's taller neighbour is known as The Chamberlin – Henry Chamberlin was another director. This housed another even larger engine which took over in 1906–7.

Every other building lies well beyond the walls. But regional supply manager Paul Naylor was kind enough to give me a tour. The first thing that strikes you is the site's sheer size. The second is that Anglian Water is clearly a company which values its history.

Inside the Chamberlin, the engine has long gone, but memories are maintained. Stern Victorian portraits of those founding fathers stare down and early record books are housed in glass cases. Elsewhere, copious records of streets and houses dating back to the 1880s not only survive, but are regularly consulted. Then, amid the fleet of four-wheel drives and the

From top: *Chamberlin and Sultzer: the engine rooms behind Anglian Water*

Paul Naylor

spare water mains, there are more modern buildings, the latest group dating from the 1990s – a time when new European regulations brought higher standards. All in all, it is 35 acres which chart the changing face of water treatment over the decades.

And this isn't just a job for Mr Naylor, it's a passion. "It's got engineering, it's got people it's got that sense of the public good," he says, "I wouldn't want to do anything else."

THE BAEDEKER RAIDS – *The Context*

The Baedeker Raids were part of a series of tit-for-tat bombings during the middle years of the Second World War. The RAF started it in March 1942 by targeting the town of Lubeck, what military historian Peter Caddick-Adams called "a pretty, medieval port on the Baltic coast of limited military value".

The aim wasn't to hit industrial targets, but to destroy homes and thus undermine morale. An attack on nearby Rostock soon followed, prompting retaliatory attacks on south coast towns like Torquay, Exmouth and Newhaven.

Then the Germans turned their attention to what Caddick-Adams called "cultural centres of no military value". These cities, the story goes, were picked because they had three stars in the Baedeker tourist guides.

Exeter was first on April 23rd, Bath on April 25th and April 26th. Norwich was hit on April 27th, York on the 28th and Norwich again on the 29th. Exeter was revisited on May 3rd. Air Vice Marshall Sir Arthur Harris responded with an overwhelming attack on Cologne at the end of May in which 45 000 people were made homeless. In turn the Germans bombed Canterbury on June 1st.

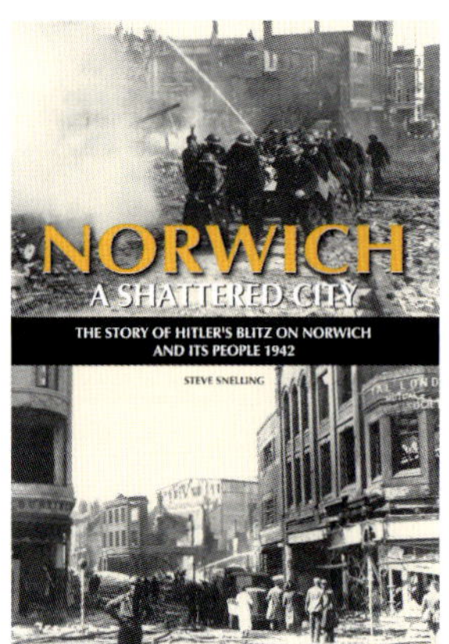

Steve Snelling's authoritative history

Norwich's Blitz

Late on the evening of April 27th 1942 German bombers swept over Norwich and all but destroyed City Station in Heigham. Both buildings and trains exploded into flames - providing an easy marker for the aircraft which followed. The north and the west of the city bore the brunt. 158 people died, a further 264 were seriously injured. Two nights later the bombers returned. This time the city centre was hit hard, but the north and the west of Norwich again suffered. People were more prepared but 67 more lost their lives and 86 were seriously injured.

The full story of what residents called "The Norwich Blitz" needs a full book – I recommend *Norwich – A Shattered City* by Steve Snelling. But it needs mentioning here because you can argue that the residents of Heigham were affected more than any other area. Indeed you can argue that the whole idea of Heigham as a place with a separate identity died as those bombs rained down.

During the war, every bomb which landed on Norwich was marked on a huge map kept by the city council planners at their offices in Ber Street. Fully six-foot square and set within a wooden frame, this map survives at the Norfolk Record Office. The location of each bomb was recorded on a tiny tag which gave the weight of the explosive and the date. Even 70 years on, it remains the best at-a-glance record of what was hit where. Heigham suffered badly – there are more than 80 tags in the area between the Wensum and Dereham Road alone.

A detail from the Norwich Bomb Map

The parish church of St Bartholomew's was left as a ruin, City Station was never properly rebuilt and The Dolphin wasn't re-opened until 1960. A shoe factory in Northumberland Street was hit, as was Barker's Engineering Works.

But it was in the terraced streets in between that Heigham really took a hammering. And this was no accident. For the Germans in Norwich as for the British in Lubeck, this was terror bombing. A folder at the NRO from April 27th 1942 contains dozens of reports from the air raid rescue units: three rescued, one body at 14 Northumberland Street; six rescued, three bodies at 65 Belvoir Street; three rescued, two bodies at 57 Helena Street; two bodies somewhere on West End Street; one body at 42 Adelaide Street.

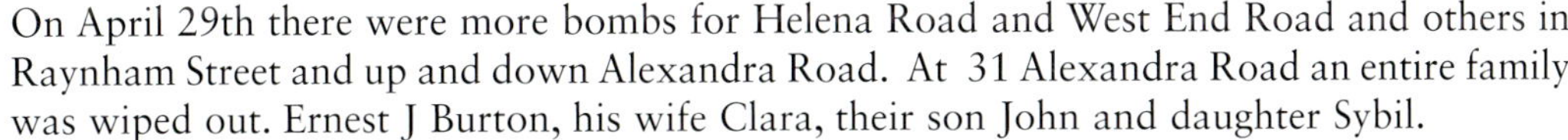

On April 29th there were more bombs for Helena Road and West End Road and others in Raynham Street and up and down Alexandra Road. At 31 Alexandra Road an entire family was wiped out. Ernest J Burton, his wife Clara, their son John and daughter Sybil.

The 70th anniversary of the Baedeker bombings in Norwich prompted a renewed wave of interest - and perhaps a slight change in tone too. Where once we concentrated on city centre destruction, now the tragedies in the suburbs started to get more attention. And since the bombings were all about terror, there is an argument that the real story, the real victims, the real heroes were to be found in the closely-packed streets of Heigham.

City Station

Imagine you're standing on the inner ring-road roundabout at the junction of Barker Street and Barn Road. Look north towards Halford's and in your mind's eye lay waste to the stores and the showrooms on Barker Street. Instead, envisage a living, breathing railway station behind a grand Italianate portico.

This was City Station, one of Norwich's three railway termini. From here a line hugged the Wensum Valley north through Hellesdon and Costessey to North Norfolk and – eventually – the East Midlands. It's hard to imagine just how vast the operation was, but those Barker

One of City Station's original platforms

Street buildings provide a clue. Take a closer look. Not one dates back more than 40 years. Everything you can see would have formed part of the 30 acres once owned by the railway – a mass of sidings and cattle pens, a goods shed, an engine shed, a coal yard, even stables.

Built in 1882 as part of the Lynn & Fakenham railway, the station later came under the control of the much-loved Midland & Great Northern line and then the London & North Eastern Railway. Its golden years were probably during the first half of the 20th century.

Certainly it never really recovered from the pounding it took during the first night of the Baedeker raids on April 27th 1942. To be fair, train services resumed relatively quickly and pre-fab buildings replaced those lost. But the grand façade was never rebuilt and I suspect the pre-war bustle never quite returned either.

After the war, car ownership boomed, passenger traffic dwindled and the station withered on the vine. The last passenger train left in 1959 and the station was closed to goods traffic in 1969. The council stepped in to build the inner ring road in 1972, removing much of the old station apparatus as they did so. In the 1980s other railway paraphernalia was buried under vast quantities of silt dredged from the neighbouring Wensum. All that remained was the trackbed, converted into Marriotts Way. Another essential part of the old Heigham, it seemed, had been consigned to the history books.

John Batley

Then, earlier this decade, something strange happened. Interest in the station started to pick up after a group of railway enthusiasts began comparing old photos via the flickr website.

Next in 2012, railwayman John Batley and a few friends started to explore the area between the river and the Halford's store on Barker Street. Having grown up in the area, he could remember what it looked like before the dredgers had done their worst.

"We started to dig and we found one brick, kicked again and found another," he said. "We knew where things ought to have been but it was still great to discover that yes this wall was still there."

What the Friends of Norwich City Station were uncovering was part of the station's Platform One – originally 660ft in length.

"Then we found some sleepers and we thought they must have just been left there, but soon you could see from the distance between them that they were original too."

With a hotch-potch of LNER memorabilia discovered and a 150ft length of platform cleared, the 50-strong FONCS group planned a walled garden. What finer way to end

Marriotts Way, they argued, than by preserving what they could of the old terminus.

Sadly, the landowners Norfolk County Council disagree. As I write FONCS doesn't have permission to carry out any work. So the group continues to patiently lobby while John leads his guided walks.

I asked the county why they couldn't agree to what seems such a simple idea. A spokeswoman responded by saying it was committed to spending more than £300 000 on the city end of Marriotts Way. So does that mean FONCS can build their garden? Err, no. At least "not at this stage, but discussions will continue".

Mystifyingly, the battle to preserve and remember the last vestiges of Norwich City Station is proving a lot more protracted than anyone would have thought.

The Bike Ride *Heigham*

Distance: 2 miles

From The Dolphin on Heigham Street take the footpath heading to Dolphin Bridge across the Wensum. Turn left on to Marriotts Way and continue for more than half a mile to a footpath crossroads. Turning right would lead you to Sloughbottom Park, but we turn left towards the Wensum.

Later, turn right at a T-junction much closer to the river, and follow this path across a pedestrian bridge which leads you up to first Sycamore Crescent and then Maple Drive. Turn left on to Waterworks Road and towards the heart of residential Heigham. Cycle past the waterworks on your left and Wensum Junior School on the right.

Look out for a small park on the right and cycle through it enjoying the remaining tower of St Bartholomew's church. Keep left within the park to emerge on to the unadopted St Bartholomew's Close. Turn right on to Nelson Street and continue until The Fat Cat pub. After drinks there, head towards the city centre on West End Street.

Turn left on to Old Palace Road. At the junction with Heigham Street, turn right for a short diversion to note a memorial on the flats, paying tribute to the crew of an American bomber which crash landed nearby in 1944. All nine men died. Turn left at the traffic lights to return to The Dolphin.

Brewers Steward & Patteson rebuilt The Dolphin after it was bombed.

Chapter 8 Norwich Over the Water

Before we get to central Norwich, we need to explore the city's less well-known quarter north of the river. Centuries ago it was called "Norwich Ultra Aquam". Today the phrase just about lives on in English: "Norwich Over the Water".

Unusually, Norwich is a settlement which grew up on both sides of the river. Most towns and cities used the water as a natural defence. But right from the early days of the Saxons and the Danes, Norwich flourished on both banks. Historian Margaret Pelling points out that even London made do with a single bridge across the Thames until the mid-18th century. Norwich had five across the Wensum by 1300. Today there are 13 including three pedestrian footbridges added in little more than a decade.

But just because this area has always been part of Norwich, it doesn't necessarily give it the same atmosphere. Over the centuries Over the Water has had a reputation for being more radical and more anti-establishment.

When Robert Kett fought the king's forces in the 16th century, this part of the city was seen as a rebel stronghold. During the Civil War it was more republican. Later the politics of its residents were seen as Whig while the area to the south was more Tory. When the non-conformist religions rebelled against the Church of England they built their new chapels on and around Colegate – Over the Water's most fashionable street.

More recently the area has felt itself to be ignored and neglected. After the Second World War, there was a feeling that bomb damage was slow to be repaired here. Its population shrank alarmingly.

By 1971 a Church of England vicar had teamed up with a Methodist minister to form the "Over the Water Group" to campaign for better recognition. The Reverend David Clark and the Reverend Jack Burton argued that the area "had been devastated successively by slum clearance, bombing, more slum clearance, movement of industry to the outskirts and finally the Magdalen Street flyover and the inner ring road".

The pressure group undoubtedly made a difference. Within months the city council had taken the (then brave) decision to approve plans for the Friars Quay housing development on the site of the old Jewson's timber yard. The balance altered. More housing developments followed, but other controversial demolition schemes were quietly shelved. The population started rising again. Today it is a happy mix of residential and retail. But does it retain its own character? I think so. Cross the river and take a deep draught of radical North Norwich air. This part of the city is less corporate, less commercial. The Norwich Playhouse flourishes on the Wensum's northern bank. Artists and designers cluster at the Muspole Workshops.

Opposite:
"Norwich Ultra Aquam" is on the left bank

I don't believe that an inner ring road killed this sense of "other". I think Over the Water has been quirkier for centuries. If anything, blame the Normans for their audacity in moving the market place from Tombland to its current location. The other end of Norwich has been smarter and richer for almost a thousand years now. But Over the Water is still going strong. Still different, still there to be cherished.

PEOPLE: *The Rev Jack Burton*

One important witness to the 1970s Over the Water movement still lives in Colegate. The Reverend Jack Burton is now a retired minister of the Methodist Church. He remains a passionate advocate for this part of Norwich.

So what makes it special? He believes Colegate itself provides part of the answer: "That street is the best in the city," he told me. "It boasts three medieval churches, two of the historic meeting houses of Europe and examples of architectural styles spanning five or six centuries – all within 500 yards."

"The Inner Link Road (added in the early 1970s) did a lot of harm to the integrity of the district, rather like slicing the top off an egg. But credit where it's due, the new housing developments have cleared up a lot of ugly and derelict sites. They've really enhanced the area."

Converted by the American evangelist Billy Graham, Mr Burton trained for the Methodist ministry between 1959 and 1963. But from 1968 he was no ordinary priest. Aware of the growing gap between churchgoers and non-churchgoers, he opted for a "worker-priest" pattern of ministry. Mr Burton was a bus driver. (Indeed he was the driving force behind a one-day Norwich bus strike, but that's another story.) He continued in this role for a remarkable 35 years until his retirement in 2003.

But is he proud of what the Over the Water group achieved?

"Well pride is one of the seven deadly sins, so no, I don't use that word. And like a lot of good things it fades as it goes into the past. The professionals will leap up and down and say they had it under control, but I don't believe they did.

"For example, our dogged representations halted the destruction of the east side of Duke Street - including the Golden Star – as part of a road-widening scheme.

"I believe the Over the Water group did a disproportionate amount of work in focusing attention on that part of the city. Lots of historic property was in a very poor condition and industry was moving out. So, pride no, but yes the thought of our Over the Water group does leave me with a very warm feeling."

The Octagon Chapel & The Old Meeting House

You don't hear the word "nonconformist" much any more. Religious freedom is so well-entrenched that the word has almost lost its meaning. Hundreds of years ago so-called dissenters weren't so fortunate. You either conformed to the Church of England or you risked your life, your liberty or your privileges depending on the century and the mood.

Yet a whole range of beliefs flourished despite the dangers. Some argued about the very nature of God and Salvation. Others argued just as fiercely about organisation and hierarchy. And, as ever, radical Norwich was at the heart of the intellectual discourse. The nonconformist heartland was Over the Water and here on Colegate lie two buildings with a rich tradition.

The Old Meeting House is the older of the two and the less well-known. It's the home of the Congregational Church, established in Norwich in 1643 and on this site since approximately 1689. In historian Vic Nierop-Reading's words they were "fervent Calvinists, believers in divine pre-destination whose building was to be a temple to an all-powerful and controlling God".

Left to right:

The much-copied Octagon Chapel

The Old Meeting House

In recent years the Congregationalists have become a much smaller group, but they still meet for worship in the same building – keeping up a remarkable continuous tradition. They are still independent too , unlike many Congregationalists who came together with others in 1972 to form the United Reformed Church. But independence and the ownership of a historic building can be difficult to reconcile – hence a deal where the council bought the building and leased it back to the church.

Further down Colegate lies another religious community with very similar roots. Like the Congregationalists, the then Presbyterians felt forced out of the Church of England by an Act of Parliament in 1662. Like the Congregationalists they initially met in a small room within the Blackfriars complex before buying a plot of land on Colegate.

But while the Old Meeting House is very much 17th century, the **Octagon Chapel** is a product of the 18th, replacing more humble buildings on the same site. Work began in 1754 and its eight-sided shape proved hugely influential. Inside and out this building is stunning.

From top:

St George's Church: Georgian splendour

St Clement's Church: Viking roots?

St Miles Church: feel the flushwork

And to me it was unlucky not to make the "Norwich 12" list of "individually outstanding heritage buildings". Perhaps if it had been the other side of the river...

Famously, the chapel was praised by the founder of Methodism John Wesley. Nierop-Reading quotes his later directions for people building Methodist preaching houses, saying that they should be "where the ground will permit in the octagon form". At least 14 towns and villages had done just that by 1776.

Today the chapel is the home of the Norwich Unitarians.

Colegate's Churches

Colegate's historic importance is emphasised by the fact that it has three medieval churches along its length as well as the two meeting houses. They are:

St George, Colegate

Light floods into this 16th century church through the beautiful clerestory windows. Unusually the church escaped modernisation in the Victorian period, allowing us a rare look at the simplicity of Georgian furnishings and fittings. Among the many memorials, there is one to the *Norwich School* painter John Crome who was buried here in 1821. St George's is now the only Over The Water church still used for worship. It's undoubtedly one of the most elegant churches in Norwich.

St Clement's

The archaeological evidence points to a Viking stronghold on this side of the river and the dedication of this church provides another clue. St Clement is the patron saint of seafarers and was very popular with the Danes. But while there has probably been a church on this site for more than a thousand years, this particular building dates back to the 15th century. Made redundant in the 1960s, the church was later rented out to the Rev Jack Burton who opened it daily for 30 years. The Norfolk Historic Churches Trust calls it "a powerful element of the townscape of Norwich Over the Water".

St Miles, Coslany

So what happens to a church after it's lost its parish? When people praised Norwich for its inventive answers to that question they often quoted St Miles. Between 1995 and 2011 the church was home to a hands-on science museum for young children. But now it lies empty awaiting another incarnation.

It is larger, probably than it ever needed to be for the size of the parish. Walk around to the south aisle. Experts praise the quality of the so-called flushwork on the exterior walls here.

Flushwork consists of different patterns of flint, all lying flush – meaning flat – to the wall. Inside it is a classic Perpendicular church with very large windows, allowing the light to stream in.

NORWICH'S BRIDGES

St Miles Bridge (Also Known As Coslany Bridge)

My favourite Norwich bridge. There's been a crossing here for more than 800 years. Earlier versions in first wood and then stone were replaced by this iron bridge in 1804. Designed by the architect James Frost, it may well be the earliest cast iron bridge in East Anglia. Frost went on to build Hellesdon Bridge later in his career.

Duke Street Bridge

The last of the ugly ones to be built and only the second to exist on this site. The first bridge was constructed in iron in 1822. Exactly 150 years later the city council replaced it with today's wider, concrete design. A more elegant bridge here would transform what is rather a morose stretch of river. Thanks to the conservation efforts of the Norwich Society, parts of the original bridge can still be seen within the entrance to the Castle Mall car park.

St Miles Bridge – the canoe view

Duke Street Bridge – why so ugly?

NORWICH'S BRIDGES *(Contd)*

St George's Bridge (Also Known As Blackfriars Bridge)

Another beauty – and the best way to enter "Norwich Over the Water" from the south. This one was built in 1784 by Sir John Soane, an eminent late Georgian architect who would later rebuild the Bank of England. A single span bridge of Portland Stone with iron balustrades, it was restored at a cost of £50,000 in 2009. There has been a bridge at this point since the 13th century. The Blackfriars built the neighbouring St Andrews and Blackfriars Halls.

Fye Bridge

Probably the first bridge to exist in Norwich. If you take the King Street/Magdalen Street axis to be the first north-south thoroughfare in Norwich then a bridge along this stretch makes perfect sense. Archaeologist Brian Ayers points to the discovery of an ancient wooden causeway across the river here. He hasn't been able to date the wood precisely, but his best guess is to the 10th century. The current brick bridge is wider than its predecessors and was completed in 1933.

Whitefriars Bridge (Also Known As St Martin's)

Probably the second crossing point in Norwich, and built soon after Fye Bridge. One theory is that it connected the cathedral to episcopal land north of the river. It gets its name from the Whitefriars priory established on the north bank in the 13th century. It was destroyed during Kett's Rebellion in 1549 when the king's forces were keen to prevent the rebels flooding in from their base on Mousehold Heath.

It was later rebuilt in first wood and then stone. The latter survived until 1924 when the council was widening the river to try to prevent a repeat of the disastrous 1912 floods. Its elegant successor was the work of the City Engineer A E Collins; proof that council-designed bridges don't have to be as nondescript as on Duke Street.

Jarrold Bridge

Over a couple of days in November 2011 three huge chunks of weathering steel were slowly lowered across the Wensum. Welded together, they formed the city's latest bridge and perhaps the most novel of the 13 yet to be built.

The Jarrold Bridge was built to connect the cathedral and court quarter to the Barrack Street development on the north bank. But it doesn't go from A to B in a straight line. Instead the bridge runs parallel to the river on the south side before sweeping across in a gentle curve. And apart from two slender columns nothing connects the bridge to the river bed.

The bridge's designer Stephen James told me: "We wanted the bridge to appear to float over the site and touchdown very lightly, rather than have a heavy footprint which might have spoilt a lovely stretch of river. The columns are effectively props and the bridge just rests on top of them without being firmly fixed to them. This allows the bridge to flex and move over the props which lean to accommodate this movement."

It's that weathering steel which gives the bridge its distinctive "designer rust" look. The engineers claim it should require no maintenance for 120 years.

Clockwise From Top Left: *The elegant St George's Bridge;* *Fye Bridge;* *Whitefriars Bridge;* *The Jarrold Bridge: complete with designer rust*

ARCHIVE: *Ancient Rivers*

So how many rivers are there in Norwich? There's the Wensum of course and the Yare. Those in the know might add the Tud at Costessey and the Tas at Lakenham. But how about the Dalymond and the Dallingfleet, the Great Cockey, the Little Cockey and the Muspole? These too were once well-known names to Norwich citizens. To a greater or lesser extent they still exist today. Hidden beneath concrete and contained within culverts they are Norwich's secret rivers. Archaeologist Brian Ayers is the expert. Most of what I've written here is culled from his excellent book "Norwich: Archaeology of a Fine City".

The Muspole ran into the north bank of the Wensum from a small pool of the same name near the modern Muspole Street. The Great Cockey emerged directly opposite, having flowed through the city centre from the high ground near All Saints Green. The Little Cockey ran from Chapelfield to Westwick Street. Downstream the Dalymond rose in Old Catton and entered the Wensum off Fishergate at Hansard Lane. Lastly the Dallingfleet ran into the Wensum between the grounds of the cathedral and Foundry Bridge.

The Great Cockey: piped in and grilled over

St James Mill

They call it the "quintessential English Industrial Revolution mill", but of course this part of the country is far from the Industrial Revolution's heartland.

In fact that same revolution helped kill the textile industry in Norwich and this elegant building represents the city's final throw of the dice in trying to help it cling on. Norwich and East Anglia had reigned supreme in this field for centuries. But then the Midlands and the North began to flex their industrial muscles. It was the beginning of the end for our part of the world. Here's how historian Christine Clark puts it:

"Mostly devoid of mineral resources and water power, East Anglia found itself increasingly isolated from technical change and innovation. ...Most harmful to its well-being was the slow decline of the worsted industry as the city was displaced by its main rival, the West Riding of Yorkshire. Thereafter adjustment was painful and prolonged."

St James Mill, on the north bank of the Wensum was part of that pain. While Yorkshire quickly took to machine-spinning its yarn, Norwich held on to the old ways. As unemployment soared, the city fathers – led by mayor Samuel Bignold – stepped in to create

St James Mill

All that remains of Whitefriars

the Norwich Yarn Company. Its first mill on Fishergate proved too small. So this second mill was commissioned. It was twice as big, but came with a hefty £70,000 price tag. The foundation stone was laid in 1836, but the project hit problems almost immediately when the industry took a downturn and many investors got cold feet.

Despite Bignold's efforts, the industry was doomed and St James Mill changed hands many times during the 19th and early 20th centuries, finally becoming the printing and publishing base for the Norwich company Jarrold in 1927. Today it houses the company's head office as well as offering space to a number of other companies.

St James Mill is also one of the "Norwich 12", a dozen buildings chosen by the Norwich HEART heritage group to showcase "English urban and cultural development over the last millennium". The buildings span the Norman, medieval, Georgian, Victorian and modern eras. St James Mill is the only one to lie Over The Water.

The mill was built on the site of the old Whitefriars monastery – established in 1256 and dissolved by Henry VIII in 1538. Today a mid-14th century archway in front of St James is just about all that survives.

Canoeing The Wensum *New Mills to Foundry Bridge*

Distance: 3½ miles round trip

The Jarrold bridge: even better from below

Park as close as you can to the Halfords roundabout in Norwich. Yomp your canoe across the ring road and along the riverside path towards New Mills – the head of navigation on the Wensum. Just downstream there are some steps to the water's edge. Float your boat and set off.

The first thing that strikes you is the uncanny absence of noise. Traffic is hurtling past the nearby Toys R Us, but on the Wensum all is peaceful. Next, as you paddle under St Miles Bridge you realise how low you are. Three-storey town houses tower over you. Further on you start to unintentionally eavesdrop on other people's lives as riverside dwellers leave their windows open. There was quite a row in one of the ground floor rooms at the art college as I drifted silently by.

Everything seems closer. Duke Street becomes St George's, becomes Fye Bridge very quickly. The Jarrold Bridge looks superb and before you know it you're sweeping past the courts and on to Cow Tower to join the hire boats south of Bishop's Bridge. Damsel and dragon flies mobbed me wherever I went and I also spotted two kingfishers in full flight. It was inner city alright, just a Broads kind of inner city.

Chapter 9 Central Norwich

Pull's Ferry

A grander, more obviously historic Norwich awaits us as we cross the river. An elegant cathedral, a picturesque watergate and an ancient hospital all lie within a stone's throw of the Wensum.

Go looking in the right places and Norwich's sheer antiquity starts to dawn on you. This is a city shaped by the Normans. Its street patterns survive as do dozens of its medieval churches. St Andrews Hall provides the most complete remains of a friary in the country. Most were ransacked after the Dissolution of the Monasteries. Here the city fathers were clever enough to do a deal with their sovereign.

Cheek by jowl with all this is one of the most vibrant shopping centres in the country. Less obvious is the city's expertise in the finance industry. We were once a city of weavers and later became shoemakers. Now, one third of the workforce is employed in the finance or business sector.

My only concern is that Norwich has yet to embrace its river in the same way as other cities. Despite the new developments, despite the new pedestrian bridges, the Wensum isn't as central to the city's soul as it should be. Is that just geography or a long hangover from the days where the river was where the poor people lived and the dirty industries were based?

Norwich University Of The Arts

Norwich doesn't do "bohemian" as such. But in the summer, when the art students spill out from their classes, the pedestrianised St George's Street gives it a good go.

There can be few more pleasant city centre campuses. St George's Building sets the tone: a four-storey block of late Victoriana dominating the southern bank of the Wensum. It was built as the Technical Institute in 1899 on land which once belonged to the Blackfriars friary. The architectural historian Nikolaus Pevsner calls it "depressing". I say "imposing".

Officially upgraded to a university in 2013, the Norwich University of the Arts has slowly colonised this part of the city. Directly next to St George's is a former middle school from the 1860s. ("Gothic and clumsily picturesque" is Pevsner's waspish verdict.) Next door again, an unusual conversion: a former Friary cloister, re-christened as The East Garth. It houses a digital darkroom for photography students. Inside the classrooms, chunks of medieval wall are encased in toughened glass. The NUA slowly morphs into the old Blackfriars complex as you work your way towards the city centre. It's not entirely clear who owns what and it's all the better for that. Previous students here include the painter Alfred Munnings, the sculptor Bernard Meadows and Keith Chapman, the creator of Bob the Builder.

From top:

The Victorian façade of the old Technical Institute.

From friary to university: The East Garth at the NUA

Utopia

When Rory Macbeth started this artwork in 2006, the bricks and mortar which formed his canvas were due to be demolished within months. Several years later the old Eastern Electricity building is still standing. So if you do find yourself wanting to read the entire text of Thomas More's 16th century *Utopia*, just wander down to the Wensum. And it is the entire text. The artist had done his homework, establishing where each line needed to be positioned so that all 40 000 words fitted.

Danger: words on a wall

"I like the idea of expressing that text through graffiti," he explained. "As most graffiti is utopian – that the world would be perfect if this or that were different."

Every brick was due to go to make way for a redevelopment in 2008. New offices, a riverside restaurant, an art gallery and apartments were promised. Then the recession struck. Redundant workshops remain – and so does Utopia. So how does Macbeth feel, now that something meant to be transitory is becoming at least semi-permanent?

"I am aware that the work has become a bit of local oddity and that some people have taken it to their hearts," he told me. "I find that really touching – and unexpected."

Utopia: all 40,000 words

Bicknell's bales

Quayside: used for centuries

Quayside

This stretch of the river has been used as a quay for centuries. But no-one knew precisely how long until an archaeological dig in 1993. Experts used dendrochronological analysis to establish that timbers found here dated back to 1146.

Today the Quayside is very much residential. And the icing on the cake for the redevelopment was an art installation of "bales" representing the different cargoes which would have been unloaded here over the centuries. Look carefully amid the 31 steel and railway sleeper sculptures and you can find names celebrating local residents and businesses.

Norwich Cathedral And Its Close

What have the Normans ever done for us? The answer in Norwich is obvious and magnificent. But before we take a closer look at the most complete Norman cathedral in the country, it's worth a glance at the wider picture.

The Normans transformed Norwich. They turned an up-and-coming market town into a regional capital. Arguably the reason that the modern city has everything from a crown court to a half-decent football team can be traced back to that key decision.

Left to right:

Norwich Cathedral from the west end

All quiet on Hooks Walk

Having decided that Norwich was to be their base, they imposed their will in three distinct areas. First, for defence, they built a castle. Second, for trade, they moved the market from Tombland to its current position alongside Gentleman's Walk. And third, for religion, they created the cathedral. Their ambition was staggering. Archaeologists are pretty sure that this part of Norwich was settled by the end of the 12th century. But that didn't stop the new rulers knocking down both buildings and churches to build a stunningly beautiful cathedral exactly where they wanted it.

Ditto The Close. We take it for granted. But at 42 acres it's one of the largest in the country. For many centuries this area was virtually independent from the city. According to historian Ian Atherton it had its own jail until 1826 and its own court until 1844. Strangely to modern eyes, it used to have its own pubs too – at least five in the 18th century. Atherton lists The Ferry House, The Gate House, Black Jack, The Three Cranes and The Garden House.

Throughout the centuries it also had its own school. The Norwich School has some sort of roots in the early days of the cathedral, but in its current incarnation it goes back to the reign of King Edward VI. An independent school, it counts Horatio Nelson (who was only there briefly, but they gloss over that) and the landscape designer Humphry Repton among its old boys.

With a river at one end, a cathedral in the middle and statues of the Duke of Wellington and Lord Nelson at the other, The Close maintains a rarefied atmosphere to this day. One 20th century dean described it as "a fine village in a fine city". Quite.

And so to the Cathedral of the Holy and Undivided Trinity. The foundation stone was laid in 1096 by Herbert de Losinga. With stone transported from Caen in Normandy (the lighter, smoother stuff) and Barnack in Northamptonshire (greyer and rougher) most of this building was built in 50 years.

The spire came later. Historian Stephen Heywood dates the first one to the 1290s. The current one – the second highest in the country – is from the 15th century.

Until the Dissolution of the Monasteries the cathedral was home to a community of some 60 monks. But the cathedral neatly moved with the times. There were 21 monks and a prior in 1538. The prior became a dean and the monks became prebendaries and canons. In other words they carried on living in the same place, but simply switched allegiance from God and St Benedict to God and Henry VIII – not necessarily in that order.

The second half of the 20th century saw major restoration work followed in 2009 by the creation of a new building. The multi-million pound hostry is built on the site of the pilgrims' guest hall and is intended to do the same job in a more modern way. Every year the cathedral holds more than 1,500 services and is visited by more than 400 000 people.

The Great Hospital: a "church" with chimneys

The Great Hospital

Look closely at the "church" above. The west tower seems normal enough and while the building is a little longer than usual, those larger windows towards the east end look in the right place too. But what about those chimneys? Chimneys on a church?

We're actually looking at a medieval hospital. Confusingly these hospitals didn't offer medical care, they offered hospitality. They were religious institutions with more than a passing resemblance to monasteries. But while the latter saw monks engage in a contemplative life of prayer, in a hospital, clerics cared for the poor and the elderly. Look again at our building. In actual fact only the middle third is a church.

The cubicle system

This complex of buildings between Norwich cathedral and the Wensum was originally called St Giles's Hospital. It was founded in 1249 by Bishop Walter Suffield. His aim was to help "aged priests, poor scholars and hungry paupers". With a blip in the 14th century – when prayers and masses all but took over – people on this site have been looking after vulnerable people for 750-plus years.

Interestingly it was the Reformation which returned the hospital to its roots. Masses for the souls of the dead were out of vogue. But the city fathers were able to persuade the young Edward VI that this was a place where the poor were looked after. St Giles Hospital was rebranded "God's House" and entrusted with the care of 40 residents. The building we see was split into three at about this time. The western third was an infirmary. The richly decorated church chancel (to the right) was converted into living quarters on two floors. Here's how one writer described them in 1947:

"In the cubicle system on its wards, you may see a happy adoption of a communal way of life inherited from the Middle Ages. And you may also see a quadrangle of houses for old married couples erected as recently as 1937. Both are models of their kind. In the big wards with their little cabins just the right balance is struck to meet both the sociable instincts of old people and their desire for some degree of privacy..."

Amazingly these cubicles survived until the 1980s. Today the institution we know as The Great Hospital has managed a complete transformation from medieval religious community to modern sheltered housing complex.

It is home to approximately 100 people. On the banks of the Wensum, in the shadow of a great cathedral, there must be few more civilised places to spend one's retirement.

Kett's Rebellion

The walk along the river from Pull's Ferry via Bishop's Bridge to Cow Tower is one of the most tranquil the city has to offer. The traffic is safely confined to the other side of the Wensum and the views across to the cathedral are idyllic.

It was less peaceful in the summer of 1549. Edward VI is only 11, so England is ruled by Lord Protector Somerset. The country is racked by social unrest. In Norfolk, the enclosure of common land by greedy gentry proves to be the final straw. In July protests in Wymondham catch light across the county. Angry men find a leader in the shape of a yeoman called Robert Kett. Kett soon finds himself leading a rebel army of 16 000 men which sets up camp on Mousehold Heath – overlooking the city.

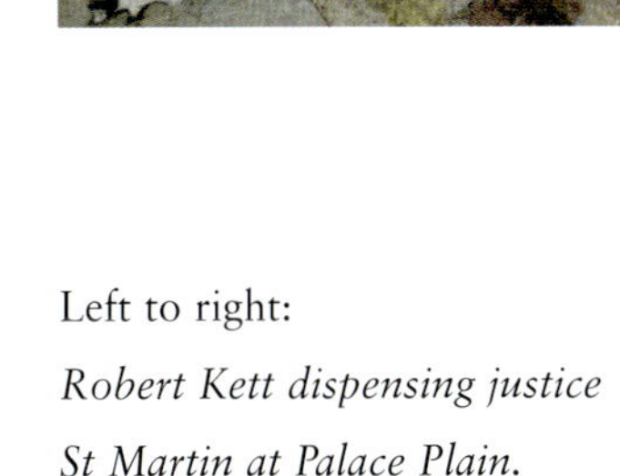

We remember it here, because this corner of Norwich played a crucial role that summer. On July 21st the rebels attacked Bishop's Bridge despite the efforts of archers posted on the bridge. A contemporary chronicler Nicholas Sotherton provides a graphic image of the "vagabond boys" helping the rebels:

"Though 'naked and unarmed' [they] fearlessly defied the shower of arrows, they gathered them up even though some had 'stuck to their legs and other parts'. Then they plucked them from their bodies and gave them 'all dripping with blood' to the rebel archers who used them to fire back at the defenders."

To complete the picture, Sotherton talks of swarms of rebels swimming across the river in an attempt to outflank the defenders. Faced with such fearlessness, Norwich quickly fell to the rebels.

Left to right:

Robert Kett dispensing justice

St Martin at Palace Plain. Dozens who died during the rebellion are buried here

Ten days later a divided Norwich was occupied by a 1400-strong army under the control of the Earl of Northampton. The Earl, sent by Somerset, secures the city defences and survives a night-time attack.

But on the following morning rebels once again storm Bishop's Bridge and head down Bishopgate towards the cathedral. St Martin's Plain was the scene of a furious battle which the rebels won. Northampton's deputy Lord Sheffield was unhorsed. He removes his visor to show he is a peer, expecting to be held for ransom. But the magnificently named Fulke the Butcher clubs him to death. St Martin's churchyard – next to today's court complex – was the final resting place for the dozens who died that day.

Norwich was once again under the control of the rebels and remained so for more than three weeks until the Earl of Warwick's much larger force arrived on August 24th. Warwick was a better general than Northampton. He held the city, despite many attacks. The rebels' stronghold was north of the river so he destroyed Whitefriars Bridge and had to be persuaded from destroying Fye, Blackfriars and St Miles bridges too. Kett no longer had a supply line to Norwich. His men were lured into open battle at a mysterious location called Dussindale. There they were cut to pieces by the brutal German mercenaries. The dream was over.

Cow Tower: a "bastille" of its day

On August 29th 1549 a service of thanksgiving was held at St Peter Mancroft church. Later this was made an annual service. And until the 18th century the church bells were rung every August 27th to commemorate the city's victory. But since the 19th century, opinion has shifted. Now Kett is seen as "part of the city's dissenting tradition". And in 1949 a plaque was installed at Norwich Castle:

"...in reparation and honour to a notable and courageous leader in the long struggle of the common people of England to escape from a servile life into the freedom of just conditions." Four hundred years after what one Marxist historian called "the greatest anti-capitalist rising in English history", Robert Kett had finally stormed Norwich Castle.

Cow Tower

In a peaceful corner of an ancient meadow lies a huge brick tower dedicated to the art of warfare. These days we call it Cow Tower, it's rather a bucolic name for one of the country's first "artillery blockhouses". Its three storeys once bristled with guns and since it dates to 1398, these would have been some of the earliest guns in England.

Before we get into the detail it's worth taking another look at why it's here. Sure, we're at a strategic spot on the Wensum. But why does it look so incongruous? Why is it quite so isolated and why isn't it part of a city wall? All questions that have been asked over the years.

The answer according to one historian at least, can be traced back to the Hundred Years War between England and France. In the latter stages A D Saunders tells us that free-standing "barbicans" or "bastilles" were thrown up directly outside city walls and filled with soldiers dedicated to beating off besiegers.

Cow Tower, named after the nearby Cowholme fields, fits this model. It had plenty of room for men and all the evidence points to facilities fit for a long stay. A solid top floor would have provided the strength for bigger guns capable of firing longer distances. The men chosen to defend Norwich might not have anywhere to run, but within a building of such height and solidity, perhaps they would have felt confident of seeing off all-comers.

It formed part of the city defences for about 200 years before slowly deteriorating. Major structural repairs in 1954 mean that old brick is helped out by modern concrete and high-tensile steel. With luck Cow Tower can stay on guard for a few centuries yet.

Bishop Bridge

The medieval Bishop Bridge survived an onslaught by Kett's rebels in 1549 only to be nearly destroyed by city planners in 1923.

With post-World War One zeal, they wanted a wider bridge more suited to modern traffic. Many local architects and archaeologists disagreed. They fought back by getting it listed. The ensuing row led to the bridge's survival and the creation of the Norwich Society, a charity dedicated to championing the city's best old buildings and promoting good design in its new ones.

Adjoining cathedral land, it's no surprise to learn that Bishop Bridge was built by the church. Today's bridge dates to about 1340, although there were definitely earlier crossings in the previous century.

Bishop Bridge: once a crucial part of the city's defences

Complete with gatehouse and drawbridge it was very much part of the city's defences. The sheer weight of the gatehouse led to its demise. It was taken down in 1791 after a survey which had shown that the whole building was leaning precariously. The bridge itself was closed to motor traffic in the mid-1990s.

From the perspective of the Wensum, Bishop Bridge is the furthest that hire cruisers are allowed to go. Upriver, us canoeists get a clear run.

A watergate, but no scandal

Pull's Ferry complete with ferryman and passengers

Pull's Ferry

It's one of the most photographed scenes in Norwich – the medieval water gate known as Pull's Ferry. John Pull was the ferryman there in the early part of the 19th century, but the building – and the ferry – go back a lot further.

In fact the story starts with the conquest when the Normans were quick to decide that Norwich would be their capital in the east. Materials for the new cathedral needed to be brought as close as possible to the building site, so a canal was dug from the Wensum directly into what would become the Cathedral Close.

In the 15th century it was decided that this canal needed protecting from water-borne insurgents – hence the need for the distinctive flint gate. Even when the canal was filled in during the 18th century, the building survived, although it did need serious renovation after the Second World War.

There had probably been a ferry here for centuries too – and where there is a ferry in Norfolk there is often a pub. The private house alongside the water gate dates back to 1647 and was certainly a pub during much of the first half of the 19th century.

But why the need for a ferry? Upstream, the nearby medieval Bishop's Bridge was protected by a gate for much of its long life. And there was no bridge downstream until Foundry Bridge was built in 1811. This is Norwich author R H Mottram reminiscing about the 1890s.

"It was one of the treats of my childhood," he wrote "to be taken across the deep, slow-flowing water, by the laconic old ferryman who 'quanted' Norfolk-fashion with a long pole, he did not row. And when landed safely on the other side, what fun to sit on the grass of the tow-path of those days and watch the slow but capacious wherries go gliding past."

Ferryman William Mollett

Norwich City started playing at The Nest in 1908. The entrance – in Rosary Road – was almost directly opposite the ferry. So for thousands of fans, crossing the Wensum by boat became an integral part of their Saturday afternoon routine.

Neville Porter, born in 1923, remembers it well.

"As a kid with my dad we'd come into the city along the Earlham Road, perhaps paying a penny ha'penny to take the tram if we were feeling rich.

"Then we'd walk through the city and down past the cathedral and take the ferry rather than walk all the way down Prince of Wales Road and then round.

"There would be a boatman there with a small punt which could probably take about six people. There were some steps on the other side and then you'd walk up Rosary Road to get to The Nest."

And so to the last ferry family – the Molletts. William Ernest Mollett seems to have taken over the ferry early in the 20th century. He ran a boatbuilding business from the same site. According to his descendants, William Mollett and wife Matilda had five children. One of them, Cecil, would become the last ever ferryman. We think he hung up his oars in 1943. Originally the charge was a halfpenny, but Cecil Mollett's wife Lily remembered that increasing to a penny during her time there.

"I used to get about £1 on a football day," she told the *Evening News* in 1977. "When the flat-bottomed boat was full it would take 20 at a time." £1, of course, equated to 240 pennies in pre-decimal times.

Cecil Mollett's daughter Dorothy on the day she married Herbert Henning

The couple's five daughters, Dorothy, Eileen, Kathleen, Gladys and Betty were all roped in as necessary. Eileen's son Gerry remembers her saying she would charge one penny to store people's bicycles and another penny to cross the river.

Kathleen was the last of the daughters to die, aged 98 in 2011. She had emigrated to Tasmania, Australia. Her niece Lesley Allard recalls that she had photos of the Pull's Ferry on her walls throughout her house. Lesley, now living in Basingstoke, feels a similar sense of belonging. "I've never lived there," she says. "But I still regard it as my ancestral home."

St Andrews Hall

Up in Yorkshire at Rievaulx Abbey and over in Wales at Tintern, tourists flock to see the ruins of buildings destroyed by the aftermath of the Dissolution of the Monasteries. Here in Norwich we have a set of similar buildings which survived that same trauma. But because the St Andrews Hall complex comes complete with roof and windows, very few people seem to realise its importance.

OK so the busy city centre location doesn't quite compare to the desolate splendour of Tintern *et al*, but nevertheless my main point holds. While the vast majority of monasteries and friaries were plundered after Henry VIII made his fateful decision, the clever burghers of Norwich petitioned the king. Specifically quoting the importance of its city centre location, they asked for permission to buy it to 'make the churche a fayer and large halle, well pathed, for the mayor and his bretherne... for their common assemblyes..." The king agreed and the rest is civic history.

As many as sixty Dominican friars once lived here. Before the Reformation these so-called Blackfriars were one of a number of monastic orders in the city. Elsewhere the Carmelites, the Franciscans, the Benedictines and the Augustinians enjoyed huge influence. But with the exception of the Benedictines at the cathedral, don't think of them as monks hidden in cloisters. Most were "mendicant friars". In other words people who preached their faith and begged for alms on the streets.

The nave of the friars' vast church became The New Hall, a venue for feasts and courts. Now called St Andrew's Hall, it is best known for its music and beer festivals. The chancel of the church at first became a municipal chapel. Now called Blackfriars Hall it's used for concerts, conferences and banquets.

The buildings which survive sprang up from the remains of a fire in 1413. By then, as historian Helen Sutermeister says, "it is clear that the furnishings of the church had departed far from the austerity advocated by St Dominic himself".

A central tower above the old nave and chancel fell down in 1712. According to Sutermeister it was "octagonal, crocketed, faced with freestone and decorated with armorial bearings... the most elaborate part of the whole building".

It's a strange but wonderful building to wander around in today. Mostly civic, with a whiff of the spiritual it is a strange amalgam. But take your pint at the beer festival or your seat at a music festival and it comes alive. St Andrews is one of the buildings that makes Norwich special.

The Walk *Central Norwich*

Distance: 1 ½ miles

Enter Cathedral Close by the imposing Ethelbert Gate – next to Zizzi's restaurant on Tombland. Keep right, soon passing the Lower Close lawn to your left, surrounded by imposing houses. This roadway becomes Ferry Lane from where you can see the Pull's Ferry watergate in the distance. Remember that the watergate was built to protect a canal. That waterway – probably on the site of today's stables – was filled in during the 18th century.

Turn left at Pull's Ferry and follow the river, enjoying the views back across the Norwich School playing fields. Cross Bishopgate, keeping the Red Lion pub to your right and continue to Cow Tower where river and path bear left. Then keep left at a fork before you get to Jarrold Bridge. This path goes to the ancient Adam & Eve pub. After drinks there, turn left on to Bishopgate and then take a right turn on to a roadway lined by flint walls. This takes you to the eastern end of the cathedral. Follow the path round to the Lower Close and then turn right to return to Ethelbert Gate... and secular Norwich.

Chapter 10 Thorpe Hamlet & the Riverside

Thorpe Hamlet: great views down to the city

By the medieval standards of Norwich, Thorpe Hamlet is quite a modern creation. Until well into the 19th century the Wensum really was a boundary for the city's eastern flank. Beyond the river lay a thickly-wooded, chalky escarpment with the remains of an old priory and very little else apart from the road to Great Yarmouth.

Imagine it in those terms and it's less of a surprise to discover this was where Norwich's martyrs were burnt for their religious beliefs. Lollards Pit was deliberately outside the city, opposite Bishop Bridge.

And Bishop Bridge was the only bridge. Neither Carrow Bridge nor Foundry Bridge existed until the second decade of the 19th century. The railway didn't arrive until 1844, while Prince of Wales Road wasn't built until the 1860s.

But as the Victorian era got into its stride, Norwich sprawled eastwards. According to the Hamlet's historian Geoffrey Goreham, the housebuilders "saw in the chalk slopes and tree-covered valleys a challenge to their ingenuity". Incidently, how many residents know that Beatrice, Florence, Ethel, Ella, Marion and Primrose Roads were named after the six daughters of a wealthy solicitor Isaac Bugg Coaks who bought this land in the late 19th century? After a supposedly worthy career he was struck off in the 1890s for defrauding his clients. The reputation of the houses has lasted rather longer.

To the south lay the factories. Boulton & Paul is long gone, replaced by the shops and flats of the Riverside development. Laurence & Scott's was another big employer. It survives with a smaller workforce under new owners. Between the two sites Norwich City FC flourishes at Carrow Road, even if much of the ground is now in the shadow of questionably high blocks of riverside flats.

Left to right:

Beatrice Road

The NR1 development: questionably high

To the north lies the ghost of Robert Kett. It might be almost 500 years since the rebel leader set up camp on Mousehold Heath, but his name is everywhere, recognised in road names and, most atmospherically, on Kett's Heights. Goreham says the water tower off Telegraph Lane is close to the spot where he dispensed justice from the so-called Oak of Reformation. The high ground has another claim to fame. It was from here that George Borrow made his famous observation:

"A fine old city, truly, is that, view it from what side you will; but it shows best from the east, where the ground, bold and elevated, overlooks the fair and fertile valley in which it stands..."

Having said that, I prefer Arthur Mee's description from *The King's England: Norfolk* written more recently.

"Here below this eastern ridge is spread the panorama of Norwich and the pageant of its history: the Norman cathedral and monastery, the Norman castle, the 30 or so Perpendicular churches, a legacy of the woollen trade, Tudor gables, Georgian parapets, 19th century factories and housing developments, a few modern factories... some stark heavy towers of post-war flats and everywhere the grace and benediction of trees."

Ah, the benediction of trees. Who can argue with that?

Kett's Heights

Kett's Rebellion of 1549 shook Norwich to the core. In the previous chapter we explored how the area between the Wensum and the cathedral was at the very heart of the action.

But to get a better sense of the rebels' viewpoint, head to their heartland. Start by climbing Kett's Hill, and half way up the hill, take a right turn through wrought-iron gates. The steep path takes you up to a peaceful spot with spectacular views over Norwich. They call this Kett's Heights and from here you get a proper feel for what was once Kett's country.

Surely all Norfolk schoolchildren should learn about this mighty rebellion? A coach trip to Norwich, a crocodile march up to the Heights and then a picnic next to Bishop Bridge to hear tales of the vagabond boys fearlessly swimming the Wensum to pluck arrows out of their enemies' bodies.

From this vantage point it makes a lot more sense. Thousands of rebels camped on what was then a vast Mousehold Heath. From here, in the heady summer of 1549, it must have seemed as if the city of Norwich was at their mercy.

Kett's Heights – from here the rebels felt invincible

But there was plenty of history before Kett. High on the summit you can find the remains of St Michael's Chapel built by the Normans. It replaced an older one dedicated to the same saint on the site of what would become the new cathedral.

By the 19th century the area had become formal gardens owned by the manager of the new gas works on Gas Hill. These works would expand throughout the 19th and early 20th centuries. For older residents of Thorpe Hamlet the smell was part and parcel of growing up.

By the time of the Second World War, Kett's Heights had become allotments. By the 1970s it had been given to the council, with local volunteers sprucing it up in time to rename it Jubilee Heights in 1977. More conservation work followed in the 1980s. Since then it's been called by its rightful name – Kett's Heights.

Lollards Pit: a grisly pub sign

Lollards Pit

Lollards were heretics. They disagreed with the medieval church's teachings on everything from the sacraments to the saints. As such they were seen as a serious threat by the religious authorities. Across the country many died for their beliefs. In Norwich they were burnt at the stake in Lollards Pit.

Heresy trials were conducted by the bishop in his palace close to the cathedral. From there the condemned would be taken along Bishopgate and across the bridge to be burnt outside the city limits. The chalk pits next to the river were ideal for this grisly purpose.

Norwich wasn't a big centre for Lollardy. But it's one of the few places in the country where the actual place of burning is still known to us today. We also have very good records of the heresy trials thanks to a particularly vigilant bishop. Bishop William Alnwick burnt at least three people at the stake, while allowing others to escape with a public flogging. The most well-known of the martyrs is William White. His name is remembered at William White Place off Gas Hill.

White had already been punished by the authorities in Kent. On that occasion he renounced his beliefs. But by 1426 he was preaching again. According to the historian Norman Tanner, his trial in 1428 was something of a showpiece.

"He defended himself with honesty and subtlety, admitting some charges, denying some, and in other cases drawing distinctions... He was forthright in his insistence on the right, indeed the advisability, of priests to marry... Notable too is the social content of his doctrine: he rejected capital punishment and the lawfulness of war."

This being his second trial, there was no escape. He was burnt, together with fellow Lollards, Hugh Pye and John Waddon.

While the Lollards were arguably a century ahead of their time, Thomas Bilney was only out by a decade or two. Born in East Bilney in Norfolk in 1495, he studied at Cambridge and became a priest in 1519. But like White before him, his sermons strayed from traditional teaching. In his view, pilgrimages were worthless, so was praying to the saints. He was prosecuted by Cardinal Wolsey in 1527 and recanted. But, filled with remorse, he started preaching again, only to be arrested by the Bishop of Norwich in 1531.

He was burnt at the stake at Lollards Pit on August 19th 1531. Exactly 400 years later The Protestant Alliance unveiled a plaque next to the Wensum in his honour. Its members called him "the spiritual father of the Reformation in England". Bilney plays a cameo role in

Hilary Mantel's masterful novel *Wolf Hall,* which chronicles this fevered time when the country lay on the brink of Reformation.

Finally there are the victims of Bloody Mary. There were many hundreds of martyrs as the Catholic Queen Mary attempted to roll back the religious reforms established under her predecessor Edward VI. The plaque mentions eight by name. But it's probable that several dozen more met the same fate in Norwich.

Again the killings were ordered by the Bishop of Norwich, a man called John Hopton who passed away soon after Mary's reign ended.

"This sanguinary persecutor of the reformers is said to have died," wrote the Victorian historian Edward Tillett, "through fear of retaliatory vengeance on the accession of Elizabeth."

Think on all that as you order a Bloody Mary at the pub which was bravely renamed the "Lollards Pit" in 2012.

St Leonard's Priory

Once upon a hill in Thorpe Hamlet there was a priory. It was built by the Normans and from there the first generations of monks must have had a great view of the cathedral emerging down in the meadows across the Wensum.

The priory sat on the corner of what is now Gas Hill and St Leonard's Road. Like countless other religious buildings it was sacked in the aftermath of the Dissolution of the Monasteries. And like countless others it was taken over by a toff – Earl Surrey in this case. The history gets a bit complicated after that because Kett's rebels occupied the building during the summer of 1549. And after that the building's fortunes waxed and waned according to whether the Surreys were in or out of favour with the relevant monarch. The family were often being found guilty of treason, which in the long run wasn't good for the masonry.

St Leonard's Priory in 1906

The photo shows the building called "St Leonard's Priory" in 1906. It's taken from some sale particulars which talk about "the ruins of the Norman Priory" still existing in the house's substantial gardens.

Apparently they included parts of a gate tower, a church and a precinct well. Mary Ash's excellent history of Thorpe Hamlet quotes a lady born in the house who remembers her grandmother seeing a ghost in the cellar. That building was demolished in the 1970s. Now two modern buildings share the site. But are there any remains left today? Any ghosts too? I wonder.

The precipitous Nest

The Nest

Norwich City Football Club has had three homes in its 110-odd year history. The first ground is still used by pupils of Town Close House School, off Newmarket Road. The third is Carrow Road which we will come to later. In between there was a 27-year sojourn at the converted remains of a chalk pit with the unprepossessing name of Ruymp's Hole.

Wisely, Norwich City rechristened it The Nest. The playing surface wasn't entirely level, the pitch, initially at least, wasn't quite long enough and some of the seating was so high as to be positively precarious. But it was here between 1908 and 1935 that Norwich City grew up.

"With its 50ft retaining wall of concrete on the east side," wrote Thorpe Hamlet historian Geoffrey Goreham, "and its soaring Spion Kop terraces, The Nest was always considered to be worth a goal start to City."

The first game here took place on September 1st 1908. Norwich beat Fulham 2-1 in a friendly in front of more than 3000 people. During their time here they would become founder members of Division Three South, win promotion to Division Two, change their strip from blue and white to yellow and green, and chalk up their record win. Crowds of more than 20 000 turned up on occasion.

But it was never ideal. And after the club won promotion to Division 2, the writing was on the wall. At the end of the 1934–5 season, the Football Association wrote to the directors to say The Nest was no longer suitable. Their last game was against Arsenal on May 6th 1935.

Old photos don't really do the place justice. There's a model in the Bridewell Museum in Norwich which puts it a little bit more in context. Perhaps the best way is to walk up St Leonard's Road and turn left soon after The Jubilee pub into Malvern Road. This terraced street once led to the ground. If you can manage to peer through the gardens, you get some idea of just how precipitous The Nest would have been.

Down at ground level it's been all change in recent years. The old home of Norwich City now provides dozens of new homes for its residents in and around Scholars' Quarter.

PEOPLE – *Neville Porter*

There aren't many people left who can remember football at The Nest. Neville Porter can. "I first went to see City I suppose when I was eight or nine so we're probably talking about 1932 or 1933," he told me.

"It was sixpence for an adult and three pence for children. I can remember standing on the concrete terracing where you could look directly down on the goalkeeper. It was all most precarious; safety considerations just didn't come into it. It was no surprise when the FA told them they'd have to move.

"I can remember seeing Willie Warnes who they'd signed from Arsenal. He was a good little winger, but when he ran he was a bit bow-legged. So all of us kids when we played football in Eaton Park, we'd all be running round with legs like that, trying to imitate him. Bernard Robinson was another one. He was one of the generation who lost out on half his career because of the Second World War."

Mr Porter, who was born in 1923, was a season ticket holder in the City Stand at Carrow Road until 2013. How many others can say they kept the turnstiles turning for 80 years?

The Riverside Development And Boulton & Paul

Picture the scene. It's 1997 and a young reporter from Anglia TV is covering plans to revive a rundown part of Norwich. The land is so contaminated that the media has to wear voluminous yellow overalls and safety glasses. It's this particular reporter's debut "piece to camera" and he looks suitably awkward, not to say ridiculous, as a result.

The soil had been affected by the waste of several decades of heavy industrial use, some of it from the railway, much more from a famous Norwich name – Boulton & Paul. Thousands worked here over the decades. Cleaned up, this land would become the Riverside development.

But guess who the young reporter was? The yellow uniform meant it would take me months to shake off the "tellytubby" nickname in the newsroom.

Boulton & Paul started life as a small ironmonger's shop in 1797. By the late 1860s it had passed through several owners to come under the control of William Boulton and Dawson Paul. A wire-netting machine on a factory in Rose Lane was one of its early innovations. It was said that the complicated equipment had to be kept going day and night to keep up with world-wide demand.

Are we learning to love the Riverside?

The company took the Riverside site in 1915, having been asked to build aircraft for the government during the First World War. Amid today's bars and apartments, it's strange to think that more than 1500 Sopwith Camels were manufactured here.

After the First World War the company diversified into more domestic but equally bulky items – everything from chicken houses to cricket pavilions. Those smart greenhouses you see in the grounds of stately homes will normally have a Boulton & Paul sign embossed in the ironwork. The company later abandoned Rose Lane to concentrate its efforts on the banks of the Wensum. Raw materials were brought up by river. Railway lines ran across the road, allowing special cranes to lift steel out of the coasters.

Steel posts with text charting the history of Boulton & Paul

The Second World War saw the company employed to make everything from factories to air raid shelters. According to historian Joyce Gurney-Read, they made about £13million worth of goods for the war effort. They were also bombed on several occasions. Making "pre-fab" houses kept them busy immediately after the war. After that there was a slow but steady downturn. The last workers were made redundant in 1986. Construction engineer Terry Haigh was one of the last to be let go. He'd joined as an apprentice aged 15, in 1958 and worked his way up within the steel section.

"It was very, very strange to leave at the end," he said. "They were a good company to work for, they always had a good reputation. The work was hard but we made the best of it and I look back without any regrets. I made some superb mates down there and there's half a dozen of us who still meet up today."

Boulton & Paul on the old Riverside Road

The site lay unused until the late 1990s when the blueprint for today's mix of shops, pubs and flats emerged. Many of us were sniffy about the warehouse bars and the could-be-anywhere design. Is time softening our opposition? Certainly it's easy to forget how ugly this quarter of Norwich used to look. What was once a miserable wasteland now hosts a supermarket, a swimming pool, a cinema and more than 200 apartments. The city council argues that it has fought off the out-of-town threat as a result.

The only memories of Boulton & Paul today are two easily-overlooked steel posts close to the Novi Sad Friendship Bridge. Look closely and you'll find text depicting some of the milestones in the company's history. It's a long way from the busy, noisy factory which Terry Haigh knew so well.

Norwich City Football Club

As a modern football stadium looms large next to even more modern blocks of flats, it's hard to imagine this part of Norwich as peaceful riverside meadows. But the site wasn't much more than that when the football club came calling in 1935. The Colman family owned the land and

Carrow Road: they love the club how much?

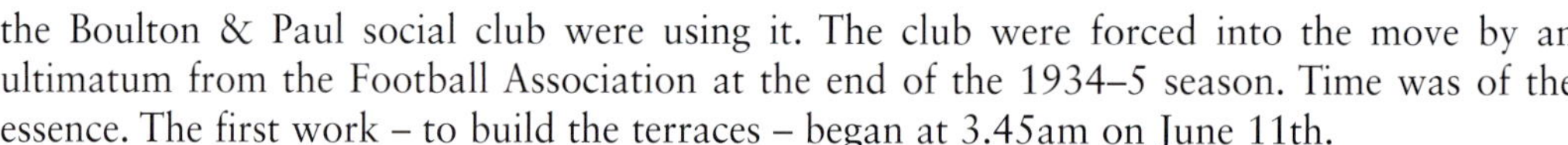

the Boulton & Paul social club were using it. The club were forced into the move by an ultimatum from the Football Association at the end of the 1934–5 season. Time was of the essence. The first work – to build the terraces – began at 3.45am on June 11th.

"The largest construction project in the city since the building of Norwich Castle was miraculously completed in just 82 days," wrote Mike Davage in his book chronicling the club's first 100 years.

"And when City officials visited the ground just before the opening of the season it was referred to as 'The Eighth Wonder of the World'".

The ground has seen a lot. Promotions and relegations of course, financial crises too. In the 1970s the club won promotion to the old Division 1 for the first time. There was a Milk Cup victory in the 1980s and a European adventure in the 1990s.

Many English clubs have moved homes in the last 20 years. Characterful old grounds in city centres have been replaced by modern stadia on the outskirts. But here at Norwich they're committed to Carrow Road, next to the river and in the heart of the city.

Now "ATB Laurence Scott"

Laurence Scott

Laurence Scott is one of the big names in Norwich manufacturing. The electrical engineers used to employ thousands at their factories hidden behind Norwich City's football ground. In their heyday they were called Laurence, Scott and Electromotors. A series of takeovers means they are now ATB Laurence Scott. But more than 100 years after they moved to this site, they are still making motors on the banks of the Wensum.

William Harding Scott was the brains behind the operation. He designed an electric dynamo for Jeremiah James Colman to bring electric light to his mill. Reginald Laurence was the money man, he became a partner in 1888.

The company soon became involved in all aspects of electrical supply – with Scott at the forefront. In a way that would be impossible these days, he threw himself at everything from early power stations to the very motors themselves.

"In an idle moment," adds the company's official history laconically, "the design department developed a mechanism for automatically controlling traffic flow at road junctions." Traffic lights would soon become commonplace across the world.

But motors were at the heart of the operation. And the famous Gothic Works squeezed in between the river and the railway, were purpose-built in the 1890s to make them. The company would add the "Switchworks" off Thorpe Road in the 1920s and expand the Gothic Works in the 1930s. All the time it was getting stuck into new markets; cargo winches for cranes, engines for diesel locomotives and a huge variety of motors for use on ships. After the war it provided gear for everything from power stations to Trident submarines.

There were some dark days in the early years of this century, but the company has stabilised since it was bought by the Austrian firm ATB in 2007. Now it employs between 180 and 200 people. And motors made the Gothic way continue to be exported across the world.

Thorpe Station

"Thorpe Station is a terminus," wrote Arthur Ransome in the opening line of his Broads adventure story *Coot Club*. He goes on to describe the watery landscape that characters Dick and Dorothea experience for the first time as they head towards Wroxham by train. When *Coot Club* was written in 1934, "Norwich Thorpe" was one of three Norwich

Still "Thorpe Station" after all these years.

stations – each one a terminus. We learnt about Norwich City in the Heigham chapter. The third station, Norwich Victoria, lay on the site now occupied by Marsh insurance brokers on Queens Road. It closed to passengers in 1916.

Norwich Thorpe lay to the east of the city because it was built to take the line from Great Yarmouth. Since the demise of Norwich Victoria and Norwich City it has taken services from all points of the compass - so lines swoop in from all directions. With the Wensum and the Yare about to merge too, the land between the station and Trowse is a complicated patchwork of rail and river which developers have struggled to tame.

The first Thorpe Station was Italianate in style and completed in 1844. The current building is grander. Indeed one post-war critic called it a "rather pompous, over-decorated building reminiscent of mediocre French railway stations of the period". Most locals today would surely disagree. Certainly it says "you've arrived" much more than it says "the end of the line".

Foundry Bridge

The first Foundry Bridge was built in 1811 and took its name from an ironworks which was just downriver from today's Hotel Nelson. A larger bridge followed in the 1840s, while the one we see today dates to the 1880s. It's so central to Norwich life today that it's hard to imagine the city without it.

Lady Julian Bridge

Lady Julian was a medieval hermit. Her book *Revelations of Divine Love* was the first to

Left to right:
Foundry Bridge
Lady Julian Bridge

Left to right:

Novi Sad Bridge

Carrow Bridge

be written by a woman in the English language. She is remembered here because she spent much of her life in a small building attached to St Julian's Church close to the King Street side of the bridge. The bridge itself was completed in 2009.

Novi Sad Friendship Bridge

Like the Lady Julian, the Novi Sad bridge is a rarely-used swing bridge. Most of this bridge rotates around the central white pier, allowing larger boats to continue upstream. The Novi Sad is named after Norwich's twin city in northern Serbia. It was opened in 2001.

Carrow Bridge

Where else would Carrow Bridge cross the river but at Carrow Road? Well it depends which Carrow Road you are talking about. The first Carrow Bridge was almost 200 yards further downstream and connected Carrow Hill to the original Carrow Road – as the map from 1920 shows.

The original road ran right through the middle of Colman's factories. Colman's didn't like that and after much negotiation, the bridge in its new position was opened by the future Edward VIII in 1923.

Technically it is a single leaf bascule bridge. In the days when large coasters came up the Wensum, many drivers fumed as the bridge was slowly raised. These days that's a real rarity.

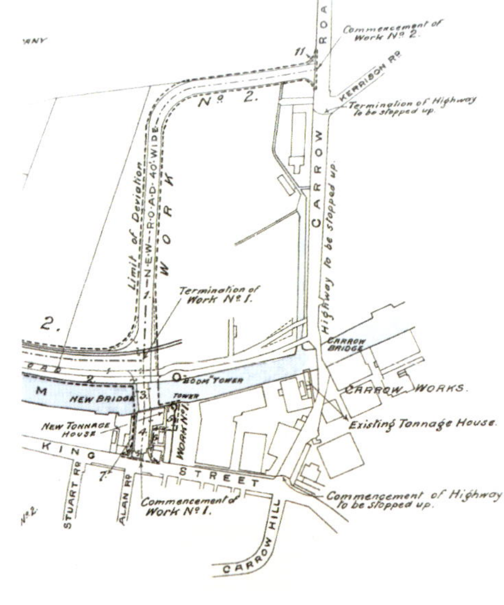

The 1920s plan to move Carrow Bridge and Carrow Road

Trowse Swing Bridge

Trowse Swing Bridge

Only river users see this bridge. But thousands of rail passengers travel across it soon after they trundle out of Thorpe Station. It's a big beast of a swing bridge which railway engineers have struggled to keep running over the years. It's been repositioned and rebuilt over its 160-odd year life – by boat you can see the remains of the original bridge just downstream. The "hangers" carry the electric current, making it one of only a handful of such bridges in the world.

Thorpe Power Station in all its 1970s glory. The more distant building dates from 1926. In its time this station provided the electricity for tens of thousands of homes around Norwich. Coal arrived by coasters. The whole complex has since been demolished. This area is now known as the Utilities Site and could soon be redeveloped. Photo from the John Chesney Collection.

The Walk *Thorpe Hamlet*

Distance: 2½ miles

From the Lollards Pit pub walk along Riverside Road, keeping the Wensum to your left and turn right up Gas Hill. The flats at William White Place are named after a Lollard martyr, while William Kett Close remembers the brother of the rebel leader Robert Kett. Robert was hanged from the walls of Norwich Castle, William from the tower of Wymondham Abbey.

Turn left at the top into St Leonard's Road but remember that the houses to the right of the junction are on the site of St Leonard's Priory. Look left for wonderful views down on to the city. After a few hundred yards, turn right into Saunders Court and follow the winding footpath through to Camp Grove – supposedly where Kett's followers camped during the summer of 1549.

Turn right on to Quebec Road and then left at the end on to Telegraph Lane East followed by a right turn on to Stan Petersen Close. At the end take the footsteps down to Beatrice Road – Thorpe Hamlet's finest street. Turn left on to St Leonard's Road and enjoy drinks at The Jubilee pub. Continue downhill and turn left along Rosary Road and then left again to enjoy the peace and tranquillity of Rosary Cemetery – the first non-denominational cemetery in the country. Retrace your steps and walk the length of Rosary Road to return to Lollards Pit.

Rosary Cemetery

Chapter 11 King Street

King Street has always earned its keep from the river it runs alongside. Today the restored Dragon Hall provides a glimpse of what life might have been like for a merchant using the Wensum during the 15th century. But just ask Norwich's older citizens and you'll hear similar tales from more recent times. Cargoes of grain, coal and timber arrived by boat until well within living memory. It's only in the last 20 years or so that this important thoroughfare has begun a slow transition from an industrial zone to a residential one.

But boy, has that transition been slow. I can't remember walking down King Street at any time since the mid-1990s and not being greeted by scaffolding somewhere and wasteland somewhere else. Breweries have been razed to the ground, new bridges built and houses have sprung up, but King Street still has a cheerfully unfinished air to it. Enjoy the contrasts while you can.

The Port Of Norwich

From Foundry Bridge down to the confluence with the Yare at Whitlingham, the Wensum once bustled with commercial activity.

This was a place of wharves and coal yards, silos and mills. Thousands of men were employed in physically exhausting work. Heading home, they would slake their thirst at any number of King Street pubs.

Author R H Mottram described it well in his 1953 homage to Norwich, *If Stones Could Speak*.

"Here, at the continuous line of "staithes", as they call a quay or landing place in Norfolk, are tied up the craft, mainly registered in London or north-west Europe, that bring to Norwich all varieties of bulky, non-perishable goods. Mills and breweries, engineering and constructional works line the banks, which, like so many things in Norwich, have never become entirely sacrificed to ruthless commerce".

To our eyes, impossibly large coasters made their way up to Norwich from Great Yarmouth. The peak year for traffic was 1936 when 753 coasters arrived carrying almost 375 000 tons of cargo. Almost two-thirds of that was coal. Substantial amounts went to a massive power station on the Thorpe bank, much of the remainder was towed further upriver – beyond Foundry and Bishop Bridge - to a gas works on the site of today's courts complex.

Bryan Read of the RJ Read milling company has detailed records for the port. By 1955 the annual tonnage was down to 208 000, dropping to 95 000 in 1973 and 55 000 in 1975.

Opposite: *Now overwhelmingly residential*

Top left to right:
A Norwegian-registered boat alongside RJ Read in 1960. "Un" weighed more than 500 tons and was 147ft long.

Alpha discharging at a Colman's mill on the football ground side

Above: *Raffelberg discharging timber at ABC Wharf*

"Once the coal-fire power station closed and the old gas-works in the city centre became redundant because of North Sea gas, the port was effectively doomed," he said.

"It hung on for a few more years because the National Dock Labour Scheme kept prices high at Great Yarmouth. The scheme wasn't in force at Norwich. So for a while it was cheaper to bring cargoes like soya bean past Great Yarmouth to Norwich and then send it back to Yarmouth by road."

In the glory days coasters carrying 500 tons or more would make their way up the Yare, creating a huge wash as they did so. Anything else on the river got out of the way, fast. Mr Read remembers the larger boats inching round into the mouth of the Yare at Trowse Eye to turn for home.

If boats needed to come into the heart of the city they could leave traffic chaos in their wake. In the days before the southern bypass, Carrow Bridge was an even more crucial artery than it is today. But if the bridge was up, motorists went nowhere.

As if in obeisance to the river's old life, the new pedestrian crossings on this stretch have been built to swing open. In reality they rarely need to.

PEOPLE – *Bryan Read*

There aren't many people left who can remember the Port of Norwich in its heyday. Bryan Read can. And what's more his family's firm was right at the heart of the action.

"I can remember what it was like, say, in 1935 when I was ten," he told me. "I would be there with my father and I remember it as a busy place. I used to love seeing the bridge lifting. I found that exciting then, I still find it exciting now.

"The gas works were up where the court buildings are now. And I can remember the coal being brought up in lighters with tugs towing them up three at a time.

"Huge boats came up the river in those days. They increased the size of the turning circle by widening the river on the Riverside Road side. That allowed longer boats to swing round before they headed home."

Bryan Read was the third generation to run R J Read, the milling company started by his grandfather Robert John at a windmill in Beccles in around 1875. In 1896 the mill in Beccles burnt down and rather than rebuild, Robert John bought an existing flour mill in Westwick Street.

A generation later, his sons Hector and Robert John junior bought the King Street site – an old yarn mill known as Albion Mills. They wanted to turn imported flaking maize from Argentina into animal feed for English farmers. They bought the land in the early 1930s and soon built a processing plant. Crucially, everything could come in by river. The Westwick Street mill moved to the same site in 1934. Wheat ground there was sold to local bakers.

As a young man Bryan Read was sent away to study engineering at university and later got experience at other firms too.

"But I was always destined to return," he told me. "In the end I came back in 1949 and gradually took over the reins from my father during the 1950s."

The company, he says, would have typically employed between 50 and 60 people. Much later it merged with Woodrows, another Norwich milling firm. The industry was consolidating. But the new Read Woodrow still had no room to expand, trapped between the river and King Street. Finally Mr Read sold up in 1985.

"I didn't want to sell, the company was in my blood. But the shareholders didn't feel they were getting a good enough return. And by 1992 the new owners had closed the whole site, so in retrospect it was the best thing we ever did."

Now he's a rare eye-witness of an era when King Street was a busy industrial landscape full of men and machinery.

St Peter Parmentergate

The King Street Churches

St Peter Parmentergate

For a big church with a tall tower, St Peter Parmentergate is easily overlooked. Despite being on King Street, it is best approached via an alley on Cattle Market Street. From there you come down the steep hill into its secluded graveyard. I love its thoroughly medieval name. (According to church historian Nicholas Groves parmenters were leatherworkers.) I also love its thoroughly modern use. It stopped being a place of worship in 1981 and has been the home of the Norwich Academy of Martial Arts since 2007.

St Julian

St Julian

Tucked away down a side alley and almost entirely rebuilt after devastating war damage, St Julian's is nevertheless the most famous church in Norwich. Indeed in terms of its worldwide reputation, it's arguably more important than Norwich Cathedral. It's all because of a reclusive medieval woman known as Mother Julian.

Towards the end of the 14th century she lay on what she thought was her death bed and had 16 visions of the crucified Christ. She was subsequently healed and many years later her *Revelations of Divine Love* became the first book to be written by a woman in the English language.

After she was healed she became an anchorite - a type of hermit living in a cell. And since the cell was attached to St Julian's church, she took that name. Her writings were almost unknown until the 19th and 20th centuries. Now she is seen as one of Britain's most important mystics.

St Etheldreda

St Etheldreda's is an ancient East Anglian church dedicated to an ancient East Anglian saint. St Etheldreda was one of three saintly daughters of Anna, a King of East Anglia in the 7th century. This church dates back to Norman times, although much of what we see today comes courtesy of a Victorian restoration. The church closed as a place of worship in 1961 and needed further repairs in the 1970s. For the last 30-odd years it's been a studio for artists. With a mezzanine floor and spiral staircases, it's a strange mixture of sacred and secular.

St Etheldreda

St Peter Southgate

One for the aficionados. The 12th century St Peter Southgate was all but demolished in 1887. But the sturdy remains of a 15th century tower survive to look kindly over a children's park opposite the Read Mills complex.

The remains of St Peter Southgate

King's Community Church

Four medieval churches are evenly spaced along King Street. But opposite St Peter Parmentergate, a different strand of Christianity flourishes in a more modern setting.

The first thing that strikes you about the King's Community Church is that doesn't look like a church. In fact from the street all you can see is a café. Inside too, it is far from traditional. It has more of a community centre feel.

Running out of room at their previous base, the church moved here in 1997 when the building was in a poor way. It had been home to the Norwich Lads Club, a well-loved youth club dating back to 1918. The church faithful had to raise £125 000 in six weeks to make it theirs. With the help of European funding they later renovated the building and helped regenerate this part of King Street in the process.

"When we first started, King Street was a red light district," explained Pastoral Administrator David Howes, "we had to escort all our lady members back to their cars." So why here?

"Well, we're a church which believes in 'insights'. One of our members had received an insight from God that our next building would be in central Norwich and it would be a building known to many. And certainly the Lads' Club ticked all the boxes."

More than 15 years later the church has 23 members of staff helping to run baby and toddler clubs, a theatre company, a luncheon club and King's Care – a service aimed at helping homeless people. Many are volunteers from among the congregation.

The main hall – home to some famous boxing matches in the days of the Lads Club – was renovated by 1998. It now hosts up to 400 people for Sunday services.

Tantalisingly for anyone with a sense of history, David puts the King's Community Church squarely in the tradition of religious dissent.

"That dissenting tradition has always been strong in Norfolk from the Lollards onwards. There's a solidness about Norfolk people. They go looking for reality. As a church we want to break free and go back to the Bible. We're not the only ones doing it and we usually keep a low profile. We just prefer to get on with it."

David Howes

King Street Breweries

Brewing has a long history in Norwich. In 1850 there were seven major breweries and perhaps a dozen smaller ones. By the turn of the century that had come down to a big four – and two of them were in King Street.

As we've heard Bullard & Sons had the Anchor Brewery near St Miles Bridge. Steward & Patteson had the Pockthorpe Brewery off Barrack Street. Then there was Youngs, Crawshay & Youngs on the site of the modern Wensum Lodge while Morgan's was slightly upriver towards Mountergate.

Morgans was the older of the two. There was certainly beer being brewed here in 1720. Beer historian Andrew P Davison reckons the tradition might go back centuries before that. The Morgan family took it over in 1845 and within a generation their "Old Brewery" covered more than two acres, while the firm controlled almost 200 pubs.

Just downstream lay the Crown Brewery of the confusingly named Youngs, Crawshay & Youngs. A John Youngs had gone into partnership with a Richard Crawshay in 1851. Youngs' younger brother Robert joined later.

According to Davison, Youngs, Crawshay & Youngs won numerous prizes for their beer at exhibitions across the country. In 1958 it was the first of the big four to close, an early victim of a consolidation craze.

But while the beer dried up the buildings have had a fascinating afterlife as part of the Wensum Lodge education centre. Opened by the county council in 1966, Wensum Lodge has become a major centre for adult education. Wander around this quirky riverside campus and you'll see a former malthouse, a stable, tun rooms and a coopers shop all put to very different uses. (A tun is a large vat used to hold beer or wine while a cooper is someone who makes barrels.)

Morgans, meanwhile, survived (as first Watney Mann and then the Norwich Brewing Company) until 1985. Almost every building associated with it was demolished by the end of the decade. Today the memory lives on only in the names of the apartments on the site; Maltsters Yard, Fuggles Yard and Polypin Yard.

In the late 1980s many would have felt that brewing had come to an end in Norwich. But the massive success of the Campaign for Real Ale means that micro and not-so-micro breweries are once again flourishing in Norfolk and Norwich. What price a hoppy smell rising from the banks of the Wensum again sometime in the next decade?

Top to bottom:

Maltsters Yard on the site of Morgans Brewery for King Street breweries

Wensum Lodge – on a brewery site

NEW HOMES, OLD NAMES

Baltic Wharf: Now a set of smart apartments off Mountergate. Once massive cranes ran alongside the river here, using railway tracks to unload cargoes from wherries. For many years around the turn of the last century it was home to Wright & Turner, "timber, deal and slate merchants".

Cannon Wharf Now 37 apartments directly next to the Novi Sad Bridge. But in the 19th century this was the site of both a coal merchants and a maltsters. In the 20th century it reverted to a coal yard under the ownership of the Norwich businessman Harry Serruys. He later converted it into a scrap yard. Many a British Rail steam engine ended up here in the 1960s.

Spooners Wharf: A much smaller development, home to just five apartments. It takes its name from the original Spooner Wharf and was very close to the site of a boat house run by the Church of England Young Men's Society rowing club at the turn of the last century.

Albion Mill: Now 38 apartments, Albion Mill was opened as a yarn mill in 1836. But the tide had already turned against textiles in East Anglia. The site was later taken over by the millers R J Read who expanded along much of this stretch.

NEW HOMES, OLD NAMES *(Contd)*

New Ferry Yard: Now home to 14 apartments, The original Ferry Yard was a slum, like hundreds of others across the city. Typically six or seven families would share one water pump. The waste from one shared toilet might be collected once a week. Landlords were dreadful and moonlit flits by tenants were commonplace. The ferry was still going in 1905. Incidentally the developers have got the order wrong here. Ferry Yard should be beyond New Half Moon Yard.

New Half Moon Yard: Now 33 apartments, once another god-forsaken Norwich yard. This yard was named after the Half Moon pub on King Street which is thought to have closed in 1885. 19th century directories list people at given addresses in Norwich, but people in yards were ignored. They really were an underclass. The only name which has come down to us is that of Frederick Allison a chimney sweep who lived at No 8 Half Moon Yard in 1912.

The Malt House: These apartments were built on the site of a pub beloved of Norwich City fans for its proximity to the ground. The Kingsway was an imposing 1930s building with steps down to a riverside terrace next to Carrow Bridge. It was demolished in 2005.

Paper Mill Yard: Just downstream from Carrow Bridge, this area once formed part of the Colman's business empire. Known for making mustard and starch, the company also tried to be entirely self-sufficient. Hence the need for a paper mill.

Dragon Hall

Norwich's best buildings have been grouped together by the city's heritage chiefs to form a sort of premier league of architecture spanning the centuries.

The so-called "Norwich 12" are a 21st century concept of course and a good idea too. The vast majority of them – Norwich Castle, the cathedrals, the Guildhall - would have made the cut whatever the century.

But not Dragon Hall. Dragon Hall has the curious distinction of being incredibly grand in the 15th century before falling into a long, slow decline. What was once a grand medieval trading hall became subdivided and neglected on a street which had also been on the slide. It wasn't until well into the 20th century that historians slowly uncovered the grand history within the attic spaces. A surviving dragon on a surviving spandrel gives the building its modern name.

But let's start at the beginning. In the Middle Ages the land between the River Wensum and King Street (then known as Conesford Street) was prime real estate.

Dragon Hall from the rear

The Dragon Hall we see restored today was built by a 15th century merchant called Robert Toppes. As such it is the only medieval trading hall built by a single merchant to survive in Western Europe. (The others were built by guilds of merchants.) It would have been a pretty ostentatious show of wealth by a powerful man.

Goods brought up by river would be stored on the ground floor and in the undercroft which survives to this day. But the timber-framed first floor was much grander. "The attention to detail and use of expensive building materials told all who walked down King Street that Robert Toppes was a successful and reliable trader" as the Dragon Hall guide book puts it.

By the 20th century it had become five small properties and one pub – the Old Barge. But somehow the fabric of the building survived both 1930s slum clearances and 1940s German bombings. Recognised as "a cloth hall" it became a listed building in 1954. But its future was only secured when it was sold to Norwich City Council in 1979. The restored building opened to the public in 1987 and was further improved before another re-opening in 2006.

The Wensum Viaduct

This wonderful vision of an alternative future for the King Street riverside comes from possibly the most famous document the city council has ever produced.

"A light and elegant structure"

"City of Norwich Plan 1945" mapped out a 50-year blueprint across 135 pages of elegant prose.

An inner ring road and an outer ring road would converge at one point, this tall viaduct "carrying a high-level road from Bracondale to the railway bridge at the junction of Carrow Road and Clarence Road."

It would be, they claimed, "a light and elegant structure of great beauty, and would command a wonderful view of the old city from which it would be seen as a terminating feature and a break between it and the commercial and industrial zone further down the river valley".

The conventional 21st century wisdom is to say thank goodness it was never built – to be fair it was controversial from the start. But I'm not so sure. In fact I can't argue with a word of it. And even if you do, remember that the inner ring road is still not complete some 70 years later. To this day traffic still crawls down King Street and across Carrow Bridge to get to Thorpe St Andrew.

The imposing Black Tower

The City Wall

We left the city wall in Chapter Six when it met the river to the south of Bull Close Road. From there, heading downstream, the river is left to do the job with a little help from Cow Tower. But on King Street, proper defences were needed, and even today you can see their remains snaking their way up the steep ground to the Ber Street escarpment.

But let's start on the river. Here, on either side, but curiously, not directly opposite, lie The Boom Towers, shorter than their original height but still imposing enough. In the old days chains were thrown across the Wensum here, first for protection and later to collect tolls. The section which climbs the hill between King Street and Ber Street looks great. Not only does much of it survive, but much appears to be close to its original height – the effect all the more marked by the dramatic gradient. There are three mural towers along this stretch Wilderness Tower, Black Tower and Bracondale Tower. Take the footpath from King Street to explore.

Colman's

"Colman's of Norwich" is still a brand to conjure with after all these years. And mustard is still being made on the vast Carrow site largely hidden from public view between Bracondale and the river.

The family business moved from Stoke Holy Cross in 1856, lured by the excellent communication links by river and rail. Within a generation Jeremiah James Colman was working his magic along a vast stretch of the Wensum.

The company was known for making starch, corn flour and a fabric whitener known as laundry blue. But of course it was with mustard that it made its mark. One Victorian writer was impressed with the enormous quantities of brown and white mustard seed kept in separate warehouses within the "manufactory":

"The brown seed (sinapsis nigra) is extensively cultivated in the vicinity of Wisbech, the white seed (sinapsis alba) is mostly obtained from Essex and Cambridgeshire. It is by careful admixture of the flour of these two seeds that mustard is produced."

That "admixture" converted a previously luxury product into a relish for the normal family. Colman's became well-known for its distinctive red and yellow livery, a ubiquitous logo and eye-catching adverts. Famously the company's profits were derived from the mustard people left on their plates.

Top to bottom:

"The Abbey"

Colman's buildings still dominate the river frontage

The Carrow site remains an extraordinary place. Its 66 acres somehow manage to encompass high-tech food manufacture, the remains of a medieval abbey and unspoilt meadows.

Of course it is not open to the public and security is tight. But head of security Mark Spires kindly gave me a tour. The original abbey exists only as ruins. But The Prioress's house, built in the 16th century, survived the Dissolution of the Monasteries by becoming a private residence

In 1878 the entire site was bought by the Colmans from the Martineaus - another distinguished Norfolk family. So the elegant building which survives today is a combination of Tudor original and Victorian renovation. Confusingly it is now called Carrow Abbey and can be hired out for conferences

Making a mint

Mark meets me at 9am. We step over the ruins on to an immaculately manicured lawn – the site of the abbey cloisters. What was once the nave of the church is now home to a 1960s canteen. And on the patio a dozen or so employees are enjoying a sunlit meal after the nightshift. Is there a factory anywhere in the country with a more beautiful view for breakfast?

In Mark's electric car we tour the site which still includes a long river frontage. In the old days the raw materials would have arrived by wherry. These days everything comes by lorry and the 66 acres are shared by two companies. In very simple terms Britvic make drinks while Colman's – under the Unilever umbrella - makes sauces. To me, the manufacturing heart still seems to belong to Colman's and like any food company there's an annual rhythm to the place. When I visit the first mint harvest has recently arrived. Fork-lift trucks bustle, reversing alarms blare and a faint minty aroma emerges from the black vats. Elsewhere there are three massive silos next to each other, individually labelled mustard seed, rape seed oil and vinegar. It's a condiments set fit for giants.

Finally a word about the early days. Historians think that Carrow started off as a hospital before King Stephen made it an abbey in 1146. Unusually it sat outside the city walls and so, in the words of authors Christopher Harper-Bill and Carole Rawcliffe, visitors approaching Norwich from the south east "could not but be impressed by the massive cruciform Norman church and walled precinct of the city's old nunnery".

Even 900 years on the remains, the memories and the heritage pack a fair old punch.

The Walk *Approach to the Deal Ground*

Truth be told, this is less of a family walk and more of a marginal trespass on the author's part into an unexplored wilderness known as the Deal Ground. It's certainly not recommended other than to approach the site, and it is included for the purposes of this book only as a curiosity, an echo of the city's past that almost certainly will disappear in time. Really, it's beyond the reach of a chapter called King Street, but because it is bordered by the Yare, the Wensum and a railway line. It escapes classification – so much so that the average Norwich citizen has no idea it is there at all.

The site itself lies along Trowse Millgate, across the railway line but before reaching the river. Near a decaying Victorian pump house lies expanse of open scrubland you couldn't imagine existing in the middle of a city.

The Deal Ground's name dates back to the days when Colman's made all its own packaging. Soft wood – or deal – was brought in by wherry and made into crates and boxes. That was all a long time ago.

Every so often it appears that the area will be developed. Every so often bold plans for houses, marinas and bridges are mooted. But so far nothing has emerged for this isolated and slightly eerie wasteland. There's no round walk as such, and for the author it' was a case of having a quick nose around and heading home.

The Deal Ground: precious little remains

Confluence

For most people the Wensum does another disappearing act after Carrow Bridge. Passengers trundle across a railway bridge a little further downstream, after that there's no sort of riverbank access worthy of the name.

So for a final view of the Wensum we need to head to Whitlingham Country Park. Here, behind the outdoor education centre you can see the confluence of the rivers Yare and Wensum.

The Wensum is the bigger river by some distance, but for some reason it is classed as a tributary of the youngster alongside. Look at it from here and the combined river really should be the Wensum.

So really Norwich is a city of two rivers. It's the Yare that runs through Bawburgh, Bowthorpe, Colney, Earlham, Eaton, Cringleford, Lakenham and Trowse. It will go on from here to grace Thorpe St Andrew and Postwick too. Enough for a second book exploring these communities and their relationship with the river? Who knows?

Confluence: The Yare (on the left) joins the Wensum

Acknowledgements

Thanks to...

The many helpful and patient staff at the Norfolk and Millennium Library and Norfolk Record Office. Also to John Alban, Nick Sellwood and Freda Wilkins-Jones from the NRO, Cameron Self from the Literary Norfolk website, Stephen Snelling, Dr Toby Davidson, Dr Neil Folkes, Bryan Read, John Downes, Mark Spires, The Rev Jack Burton, The Rev Darleen Platt, The Rev Enid Jones-Blackett, Paul Naylor, Juliet Webster, Alison Yardy, Katy Walters, Rob Brown, Boaty Granny, David Howes, Nick Williams, Les Bicknell, Rory Macbeth, Niki Tansley, Jon Sadler, Dick Lubbuck, Sue Simpkin, Paul Clarke, Joyce Chesney, Stephen James, Richard & Bridget Belson, Karen Woodhouse, Keith Briggs, Stuart Henning, Gerry Bullard, Lesley Allard, Neville Porter, Julie Hay, Bernard Rose, Reggie Kent, David Harris, Terry Haigh, John Butcher, Michael Fitt, Roy Howard, Alfred Cossey, Martin Wyatt, Dave King, Tim Green, Sue Haney and John Batley.

Debbie Tubby, Shaun Whitmore, Tony Campbell, Joseph Mason, Hilda Kaye and Stuart McPherson helped with their expertise on particular chapters. Mum and Caroline were once again happily roped in for their excellent proof-reading skills while Dad tried to keep me on the straight and narrow on railway matters.

Thanks to Therese Nelson and Maria Meere for their permission to publish the Gale Force poem by Francis Webb.

Thanks too to everyone at Halsgrove, especially Simon Butler.

Photos:

Thanks to the following for permission to use their photos.

Ringland: Sir Alfred Munnings, Sir Alfred Munnings Museum, Dedham. **Taverham**: William Marriott, the William Marriott Museum. **Drayton:** RG Carter, R G Carter Archive; Ernest Raikes, Oliver Dashwood collection; archive pub photos, Joseph Mason; Francis Webb, Dr Toby Davidson. **Hellesdon:** Aerial photo, Tim Green at Briar Chemicals. **Mile Cross**: Edwards & Holmes, Stuart McPherson; Dick Lubbuck, Jon Sadler. Stuart McPherson, Stuart McPherson. **Heigham:** Swan Baths Norwich and archive swimming lesson photo courtesy of Norfolk County Council Library and Information Service; Swan members at Eagle Baths, Richard & Bridget Belson; Norwich bomb map detail, Norfolk Record Office Acc 2007/195. **Over the Water**: Rev Jack Burton from Rev Jack Burton. **Central Norwich**: The Great Hospital from The Great Hospital collection. Pull's Ferry archive photos, Stuart Henning. **Thorpe Hamlet:** St Leonard's Priory, Norfolk Record Office MS4436, 38B7; Boulton & Paul, courtesy of Norfolk County Council Library and Information Service; Carrow Road map, Norfolk Record Office N/EN 26/8; Thorpe Power Station, the John Chesney collection. **King Street**: Port of Norwich archive, Bryan Read; Wensum Viaduct, Stuart McPherson

Select Bibliography

An Artist's Life, A J Munnings; AJ – The Life of Alfred Munnings, Jean Goodman; An Illustrated History of Taverham, TB Norgate; Taverham Paper Mill, Ernest Gage; Forty Years of A Norfolk Railway, William Marriott; South Lynn to Norwich City, Richard Adderson and Graham Kenworthy; The Archaeology of the Landscape Park, Tom Williamson; In Search of St Walstan, Carol Twinch; Something about Drayton, Madeline Checkland; Collected Poems – Francis Webb, Dr Toby Davidson; Where Elephants Nest, Peter J Beer; Oxford Dictionary of Saints.

Costessey – A Look into the Past, Ernest Gage; Costessey Hall – A Retrospect, Ernest Gage; Old Costessey: A Study in Village Settlement, Anon; The History of Costessey, TB Norgate; Notes on the History of St Mary's Church, Hellesdon, Freda Wilkins-Jones; Hellesdon Past and Present, RS Joby; A History of Hellesdon Village, Kenneth Hipper; The Land Use, Ecology and Conservation of Broadland, Martin George; Milestones to Mile Cross, Mile Cross History Research Group; Heigham Street, Women's Oral History Project; Heigham – Vol 40, Edward Tillett; Heigham, Development of a Norwich Suburb, John Belcher; A New History of the Parish of Heigham, James Akehurst; Gibraltar Gardens, Geoffrey Kelly; The Dolphin, Geoffrey Kelly; Bishop Joseph Hall, Frank Livingston Huntley.

The Church Over the Water, The Rev Jack Burton; Shoemaking in Norwich, WL Sparks; Norwich in the 19th century, Christopher Barringer; Norfolk1: Norwich and North East, Nikolaus Pevsner and Bill Wilson; Norwich: A Fine City, Bryan Ayers; Tudor and Stuart Norwich, John Pound; A History of Norwich, Frank Meeres; Norwich since 1550 Carole Rawcliffe and Richard Wilson; If Stones Could Speak, Ralph Mottram; A Prospect of Norwich, George Nobbs; Norwich through the Ages; James Wentworth Day; Norwich 12 – a journey through the English city, Norwich Heart; The Blue Plaques of Norwich, Nick Williams; Norwich City of Industries, Nick Williams; The Story of the Norwich Boot and Shoe Industry, Frances and Michael Holmes; City of Norwich Plan, C H James and S Rowland Pierce; Coastal Shipping Magazine – article by Barry Bridges; Norwich at Peace, Joan Banger; Norwich: The Ordeal of 1942, E Le Grice; An unlikely Rebel, Adrian Hoare; Revolt of the Peasantry, Julia Cornwall; The Greyfriars of Norwich, Richard Hale and Mary Rodgers; Norwich Cathedral Close, Roberta Gilchrist; Two classical Non- Conformist Chapels, Vic Nierop-Reading; Business, Tact and Thoroughness, David Jones; The Norwich Blackfriars, Helen Sutermeister; Norwich Cathedral, Church, City and Diocese, Ian Atherton et al; A Short History of the Great Hospital, Elaine Phillips; The Medieval Churches of Medieval Norwich, Nicholas Groves; The Best of Jonathan Mardle, Eric Fowler; Mousehold: A short history, Geoffrey Goreham.

The Norfolk and Suffolk Broads, Robert Malster; Wensum River Parkway, The Norwich Society; Heritage over the Wensum, Norwich City Council; Land of the Broads, Ernest Suffling; Memories of Thorpe Hamlet, Mary Ash; Thomas Bilney of East Bilney, Eric Whitwell; The Later Lollards, John Thomson; Canary Citizens, Mike Davage; Justly Celebrated Ales, Andrew P Davison; The History of Colman's – Educational Guide; Seventy Years Young, a History of the Norwich Lads Club; Carrow Abbey, SH Edgar; The Churches of King Street, Richard Hale.

Finally, and invaluably, the online NHER records from Norfolk Record Office.